CAPITAL FOR KEEPS

CAPITAL —FOR— KEEPS

Limit Litigation Risk While Raising Capital

RUSSELL C. WEIGEL, III

NEW YORK

LONDON • NASHVILLE • MELBOURNE • VANCOUVER

CAPITAL FOR KEEPS

Limit Litigation Risk While Raising Capital

The legal content of this book is accurate as of July 1, 2017.

Published in New York, New York, by Morgan James Publishing. Morgan James is a trademark of Morgan James, LLC. www.MorganJamesPublishing.com

The Morgan James Speakers Group can bring authors to your live event. For more information or to book an event visit The Morgan James Speakers Group at www.TheMorganJamesSpeakersGroup.com.

ISBN 978-1-63047-451-5 paperback
ISBN 978-1-63047-452-2 eBook
ISBN 978-1-63047-453-9 hardcover
Library of Congress Control Number:
2014917775

Cover Design by:
Rachel Lopez
www.r2cdesign.com

Interior Design by:
Bonnie Bushman
The Whole Caboodle Graphic Design

In an effort to support local communities, raise awareness and funds, Morgan James Publishing donates a percentage of all book sales for the life of each book to Habitat for Humanity Peninsula and Greater Williamsburg.

Get involved today! Visit
www.MorganJamesBuilds.com

Dedication

To the Entrepreneurs in the USA Seeking to Raise Capital:

"Plans fail for lack of counsel, but with many advisers they succeed."
Proverbs 15:22 (NIV).

Table of Contents

FOREWORD
by Wayne Allyn Root

I've had the pleasure to know Russell, and one thing is clear, he is on a mission to protect America's business community and support our economy. These are goals that I share.

As the *Capital Evangelist*, a serial entrepreneur, CEO, best-selling author for business books, and a defender of small business, I believe that if Americans are not generating new businesses and expanding existing businesses, our independence as citizens and as a country are at risk.

America's solution is simple: if we want jobs, then businesses need to raise capital, prudently allocate the proceeds, and get to work. Raising capital, therefore, must be done with knowledge of the rules and regulations—and there are a maze of them that carry hefty penalties for non-compliance. Russell Weigel's book *Capital For Keeps* will help business executives and entrepreneurs traverse the maze. It provides a wealth of information on the means available to businesses to raise capital properly. "Capital for keeps" means your company doesn't have to give it back (or suffer worse outcomes) because of an avoidable error.

Russell is a practicing securities lawyer who both defends executives from investor and government securities cases and also assists companies in raising private capital and in taking their companies public. *Capital For Keeps* employs the guidance and insights of Russell's twenty-five years of concentrated legal experience by highlighting: the legal risks associated with raising capital and the consequences of doing it incorrectly, the benefits of planning and consulting with experienced professionals, and a path to limit litigation risk.

Enjoy the book—and don't try to raise capital on your own!

—**Wayne Allyn Root**
Henderson, Nevada

FOREWORD
by R. Richard Hawkins, II

I first met Russell in a downtown hotel in Miami, Florida, in late March 2008. Prior to that time he was just a voice on the phone. He was introduced to me through some professionals that we both had done work for in the past. For those of you that are not familiar with downtown Miami, there is a small tram that runs only through the downtown area of the city. I saw Russell get off of the tram, not knowing it was Russell at the time, and watched him walk a half a block down to the crosswalk to cross the street and a half a block back so he could enter the hotel. The hotel entrance was directly across the street from the tram station.

After realizing that the man that I saw walk that half a block to the crosswalk and half a block back and not jaywalk across the street was Russell Weigel, I thought to myself, "This is the man that I want representing my SEC audit clients." Those of us who play in the arena of public company work are familiar with the many pitfalls that our clients can fall into. I want an SEC counsel for my clients who "has never jaywalked in his life, he is so law-abiding."

Since that first day, I have referred any and all contacts to Russell for his counsel. I am happy that I have done that and I am happy that he is the kind of attorney and man that is needed in this perilous arena that we have entered to make our living.

It is said that the world judges us on our actions while we judge ourselves on our intentions. To me, true integrity is judged by what we do when no one is watching our actions.

—R. Richard Hawkins, II, CPA
Los Angeles, CA

ACKNOWLEDGEMENTS

This book is the direct result of my friend and mentor, Steve Pohlit. It was his idea that I put down on paper my knowledge and experience for the benefit of mankind. Without the sustained emotional support of my wonderful wife, Luz, this mental pregnancy could not have endured. Will she put up with the writing of another book?

My dad, Dr. Russell C. Weigel, Jr., my uncle, Dr. Richard D. Weigel, and his wife Leslie Weigel, and Victor Menasche, all provided great commentary. My dad spent a considerable amount of time on the book. He treated the book as one of his Ph.D. student theses and edited it with similar critical analysis. The product is much better as a result.

My heartfelt thanks go to Robert and Elizabeth Fountain for their moral support and encouragement, and to securities attorney Adam Turk and CPA and author Ted Felix for their technical reviews. Their incredible guidance and support helped to make this book possible.

As always and foremost, I thank God.

—Russell C. Weigel, III

INTRODUCTION

There are books on how to raise capital, how to crowdfund, how to find angel or venture capital, etc. This is a different kind of book. This book is about staying out of jail. It is about legal survival. It is about prudence. *Capital for Keeps* is about avoiding the errors that can force you give up the capital that you raised and more.

Entrepreneurs seek and raise capital every day. Many entrepreneurs blindly seek capital from others, completely oblivious to the strict laws that apply to this activity. So many people are doing it incorrectly-making general solicitations for investments and advertising investment opportunities-that many people assume that it is okay to seek capital in that manner. It is not okay. In fact, under both state and federal law, the failure to adhere to strict investment or securities offering registration requirements can give rise to both criminal and civil liability for those participating in the improper investment solicitation. In August 2013, I attended a micro-finance-networking event that included potential investors, real estate entrepreneurs, inventors, certified public accountants, attorneys, and start-up company representatives. I attended for the purpose of networking to generate deal flow for my law firm. I had never been to one of those events and was shocked at how blatantly start-up company representatives were permitted to showcase their companies and to pitch to prospective investors that they had never met and had never qualified. Most of the companies were seeking less than $150,000 and some as low as $30,000. Indeed, I was also surprised that the organizer of the event would help answer questions from the crowd and would express his personal knowledge about the enterprise that was making the pitch. In every situation he validated the bona fides of the company seeking money to the crowd. I suspect that this kind of situation goes on every day across the country. In fact, when I remarked to a couple of folks that I was surprised how this event was being conducted, one of them said to me, "People do this all the time. They do it on 'Craigslist' all the time. Are you telling me that that isn't legal? "

Yes, I am.[1] While I do not know whether anybody in that event was properly licensed to sell securities, no disclosure was made about whether anyone was licensed as a securities broker or whether anybody involved was being compensated for introducing or sponsoring the companies that were showcased. As far as I could tell, the companies seeking investment had no prior business relationship with most or all of the potential investors in the crowd. Although there were some attorneys who appeared to be regular participants as potential investors at these events, the attorneys did not seem concerned or cognizant that they were witnesses to potentially illegal securities offerings, and their obvious presence in the audience might have provided false comfort to the organizers and capital seekers. Indeed, no one there seemed to have any knowledge of the legal risks they were engaging in by seeking capital in this manner. No one qualified *me* as to whether I was financially suited to engage in inherently-risky investments in start-up companies. Maybe they let me in because I have grey hair.

But this is the economy that we live in today. I am not rationalizing or condoning noncompliance with legal requirements because of a need to survive. The fact is that bank financing simply is not available to start-up companies or entrepreneurs whose businesses are not cash flow positive. So the only way small companies and entrepreneurs can obtain capital is from potential investors. The cost of obtaining capital from non-bank sources can be very expensive. For example, investment banking or hedge fund capital typically is not available to start up companies. These institutions are looking for bigger deals with less risk

1 Prior to September 22, 2013, general solicitation of investors without a securities registration statement having been declared effective by the appropriate securities regulator was illegal.

and higher returns than the start-up company market can offer. They may also have programmatic limitations on the percentages of any one company that they can own. Thus, they cannot invest much money without owning a large chunk of a small company, which prevents them from making any investment in a small company. Venture capital might be available, but venture capitalists often insist on owning up to 50% or more of the company in exchange for their investment dollars and typically demand an exit strategy for their investment dollars. Venture capitalists also may insist on serving as the company's accounting department so that they can ensure that their monies are only used for permissible purposes. This makes them highly involved and perhaps puts them in control of the company's cash flow. Many businesses simply do not want to give up control to strangers. That leaves friends and family, pre-existing business relationships, and the general public, as potential investment sources. Before the September 2013 effectiveness of the rule that allowed "advertised private offerings,"[2] unless the investment offer was registered appropriately under federal or state law or both, then a solicitation of an investment opportunity to people that you do not know was invariably illegal. The temptation and perhaps individual need to solicit funds from the general public is obvious because there are simply so many people out there who can be solicited. How wealthy are your friends, family, and pre-existing business relationships? For many entrepreneurs, these known persons lack the capital to contribute to the enterprise. They are not a realistic option.

So, you ask, what can possibly go wrong? Frankly, deals do blow up. Companies fail every day. We live in a litigious culture. Personal liability for fraud, misrepresentation, unregistered securities sales, and unlicensed securities broker activity is the law in every state. Litigation is a possibility in every investment deal unless steps are taken to minimize the possibility of, or the possibility of the success of, such reputational-damaging allegations. Would you expect to be sued for *securities fraud* when your real estate investment goes south? How can that be avoided or the risk made more limited? Such legal theories can be and are thrown at entrepreneurs and corporate management every day in attempts by investors to recoup their investments and shift their losses back to the investment promoter and issuer.

2 The SEC declared Regulation D Rule 506(c) effective, which permits general solicitation of accredited investors not previously known to the issuer.

In this book I attempt to show the entrepreneur and small company executive how to limit litigation risk while raising capital. Nobody can always predict the future accurately. If you knew your deal was going to explode, you would have taken steps in advance to minimize the consequences. Planning is everything. Prepared people persevere. There is a map to the minefield. What is the safest route? "Safe" means limiting your legal exposure because every capital raising event has potential legal exposure and consequences. In essence, you can seek investment funds from others in a legally compliant manner and reduce the risk of civil or criminal litigation from investors, securities regulators, and criminal authorities.

While no book can be a substitute for competent professional advice and counsel, if you are made aware how you can raise capital in a legally compliant way, you will be able to make better decisions about your own abilities and whether and when to seek professional assistance. Know also that the securities laws will not allow you as the executive of the issuer to shift blame on your advisors and counselors. Your name is on the dotted line. You are personally responsible.

If you are an entrepreneur or small company executive seeking investment funds for your business, to buy other companies, or to finance a real estate or other business acquisition, this book is for you.

Chapter 1

RAISING CAPITAL

An Overview of the Regulation of Investment Offerings and the Risks of Non-Compliance

Gaining access to inexpensive cash financing to leverage a business or business opportunity is the eternal quest of the entrepreneur and the small business executive. Since bank financing has not generally been available since 2008, businesses needing money often can only turn to private or public investors for investment funding. Most small company executives and entrepreneurs are oblivious to the fact that when they seek money from passive investors, they have created an investment "security."

A security can be something as common as company stock or a savings bond. A security can be a promissory note, a guaranty, any oral or written arrangement where an investor tenders her funds to another person or entity with the understanding that the recipient will perform a service to generate profits for the investor, including the pooling of investment funds to buy out a life insurance policy, to invest in an emu egg farm, to participate in a multi-level marketing program, or to have an interest in a condominium rental pool. All involve the hope of earning passive investment income. All of these are securities, and securities are heavily regulated by state and federal law.

What does this have to do with a business or real estate entrepreneur seeking investors? Legally, everything. Unless you are the United States of America and you are offering United States treasury or savings bonds, or you fit into one of ten other federal special statutory exemptions, all securities offers must be registered. What does registered mean? A registered offer is one filed with the U.S. Securities & Exchange Commission and/or filed with the state securities commission where the investor is located. A registered offer is referred to as a "registration statement." A registration statement is a disclosure document that describes the issuer of the securities investment, the terms of the offering, the risks of the business and its industry and the risks of the investment, and discloses the actual or projected financial performance of the issuer, describes its management and their backgrounds, and many other details about the issuer. The first registered offer of an issuer of securities is often referred to as its initial public offering (IPO).

Because there are statutory exemptions for specific offering situations, most investment offerings are conducted as private offerings (also known as private placements) and are not registered. Generally speaking, private offerings are less expensive for companies to undertake because they do not undergo federal government review before being made available to prospective investors. Depending on the nature of the offering and the statutory exemption travelled under by the issuer, state securities commission registration may still be required for certain offerings.

The primary distinction between a public offering and a private offering is that public offerings are offered to the general public without regard for the knowledge level or sophistication of the prospective investors because they are receiving a disclosure document that has been filed with the government. Whereas, until recently federal law prohibited private (unregistered) offerings from being solicited or advertised because no disclosure document would have been filed or reviewed by the appropriate securities regulator, unless an applicable state statute authorized local advertising. The failure of an issuer to comply with the exemption requirements always has meant that it conducted an illegal unregistered offering. People have been jailed for such violations because the solicitation to sell an unregistered, non-exempt, security is punishable as a felony at the state and federal level.

Small companies face the possibility that their registered solicitations for investment funds must be registered at both the federal level and in each state: (i) where they propose to offer an investment, and (ii) where the offer originated. The exemptions are tricky, but, in certain circumstances and in a few states, it is possible to advertise an investment solicitation if the offer is limited to the residents of a single state, and the solicitation is conducted in compliance with that state's law. However, state offering registration may be a requirement before in-state advertising is permissible.

Attaining an exemption from registration for a private unregistered securities offering generally depends on how much money is being raised and whether the investors are accredited or unaccredited. Generally speaking, accredited investors have at least one million dollars of net worth (excluding the value of their primary residence), or they have two hundred thousand dollars in income (or three hundred thousand dollars combined with the spouse's income) counting backwards from the date of the investment and going back two years. Unaccredited investors, therefore, are everybody else.

The state and federal securities laws are designed to protect the investor, but not you, the issuer. Failure to comply with the registration requirements automatically means that the issuer and those involved in the distribution of the illegal offering are strictly liable. There is no legal defense to an unregistered securities claim except that the offering met the requirements of an exemption from registration. It is the issuer's burden to prove that the offering complied with at least one applicable registration exemption. Most often, issuers are unable to qualify for an exemption if they have conducted an offering without prior planning to qualify for an exemption.

The consequences of failing to register an offering depend on who is coming after you. An unhappy investor can sue for rescission of the investment plus statutory interest, costs, and attorney's fees. If the company cannot rescind the investment because it lacks sufficient funds, the investor can seek and obtain joint and several rescissionary damages against all officers and directors and those participating in the offering on a personal basis. As a general proposition though, most investors will not sue to unwind a deal unless the deal has blown up in some aspect. A state securities commission or the SEC can sue for disgorgement and penalties and obtain injunctive relief, whether or not your deal blew up. Having rescinded all investors' investments is not a defense to an SEC enforcement action, but it may serve as a defense to a state securities commission action. State and federal criminal agencies can and have criminally prosecuted those involved in an unregistered securities distribution. Of course, fines and incarceration are potential remedies in a criminal proceeding.

If fraud or negligent misrepresentation is alleged against you, the civil remedies can include all that are available in an unregistered securities claim. In a fraud case brought by the SEC, the SEC can seek to bar officers, directors, and those alleged to be controlling persons from serving as officers or directors of public companies and bar them from participating in an offering of penny stock (typically a stock priced less than five dollars per share). In criminal cases, at the state level, a negligent misrepresentation is a criminal offense. At the federal level, only an intentional misstatement or omission of material fact or one made or omitted while acting willfully blind to obvious circumstances will suffice for criminal liability. At the federal level, punishment depends on many factors including how much money is alleged to have been lost in the overall scheme. Federal incarceration for securities violations can be up to twenty-five years per violation.

The point is that most people are unaware that if they are seeking investors' funds they are invoking the securities laws into their deals and personal affairs. For example, a savvy real estate investor could sue under the securities laws to get out of his pooled real estate investment claiming that he hadn't been provided a state-required securities disclosure notice. If an investment is not performing the way the investor hoped, or if she simply wanted her money back to spend on something else, she might look to the securities laws to find some technicality on which to build a claim for rescission. It can and does happen. You, the issuer, can be insulated from some of this with proper planning. Even if you are aware, I can tell you all day what to do and not do, but if you or your staff or your brokers execute poorly or improperly during the live offering, you risk exposure to everything I have just warned you about.

Furthermore, who are the investors you accepted money from? What do you know about them? Are they friends of friends but strangers to you? Are they litigious? The character of the investors you let into your company or into your deal can be an issue that keeps you awake at night. For whatever reason or no reason, investors can decide to threaten to sue you and your company to pressure you to let them out of their investment. I have seen it happen. Being confident that your deal documents are sound helps a lot with your sleep habits. But any investor at any time can complain to the SEC and state securities regulators. Usually when that happens the investor is hoping to bring you and your company down for free, i.e., not paying an attorney to threaten you. Most often, the SEC will not respond with any meaningful action unless there are multiple complaints, or the apparent dollar amounts of the offering are over one million dollars, or the matter appears to be prominent or likely to be prominent in the news media. If you get a letter from the SEC, take it very seriously and seek counsel immediately.

The warning I am giving seems inconsistent with the experiences of many people. You may wonder, "Why are people advertising private offerings on Craigslist or on the internet or in the classified section if these are illegal?" "Isn't everyone raising money this way?" There are several reasons. One reason is that there are *only* fifty state securities commissions, plus Puerto Rico, and twelve SEC offices that are on the front lines of policing the advertisement of private securities offerings. It is simply a numbers game. Let me give you an example. Back when I was an enforcement chief at the SEC, I remember being at a management retreat where some staff members demonstrated a live-feed of emailed offerings—stock touts—coming to a government email address. There were about 90 in one minute. We were dumfounded how to curb this activity, which we perceived as being baseless and fraudulent. But that was around 1996, and the SEC was way behind the curve in policing the nascent internet. My point is that it is a numbers game, and much of the riff raff may simply go uninvestigated because the government resources are overwhelmed. Since 1996, greater government resources have been allocated to police the electronic marketplace.

Another reason is that the public does not inherently know what is legal or illegal. There is nothing inherently immoral about conducting an offering of securities. No one that I have heard of gets a visceral reaction to "common stock."

Sure, I get that reaction occasionally from people when they discover that I am a lawyer! I am sure some other professions do, too. Maybe people get a gut-turning reaction when the words "Wall Street" or "Madoff" or "stockbrokers" are mentioned. In contrast, most people perk up at the mention of an investment opportunity, I have noticed. But people tend to operate with their common sense in most daily activities. I do not think most people spend their idle time memorizing statutes and regulations so that they can be sure to know the law, which they are presumed to know anyway. I don't think most lawyers do that either. There isn't time in this era of information overload.

Other possible reasons for the plethora of advertised unregistered investment opportunities are that people mimic what other people do, and Craigslist does not warn the public about the illegal nature of their advertising content. It is how we learn when we are infants and toddlers, by mimicking, and we get by with it. Although the SEC and the state securities commissions do a good job in general of cataloging and publishing on the internet the names of everyone they have sued, they do a poor job of educating the public on what the rules are. I should note that SEC Chairman Arthur Levitt, Jr., during the mid-1990s conducted a series of investor town hall meetings to educate people about securities fraud, the targeting of the elderly, and the resources available to the public. These outreach efforts were novel for the SEC and in my view served as a great example of what executive branch government can do if its goal is to educate and serve as a public resource and help investors make wiser investment decisions. Chairman Levitt remains a hero in my book for his approach to government. Nevertheless, these town hall meetings were designed to benefit investors, of course, because part of the SEC's mandate is to protect investors. No government agency has the mandate of trying to help *issuers* conduct securities offerings properly. That's why securities issuers need lawyers to guide and protect them.

Here is a typical small company example:

Mary is the owner of a successful nail care business. She believes that she can expand her business to a couple of new locations but also may be able to acquire one or two of her competitors for the right amount of cash. However, Mary does not have the cash in her business to expand this quickly. Mary has seen that some businesses have advertised in local classifieds for investors. That gives her an idea. She knows that many of her customers seem to be wealthy, so she puts a small flyer by the cash register that says, "We are growing. Wouldn't you like to be part of our future? Contact Mary for more information."

Can she legally seek capital this way? The answer is no, unless she is prepared to file the required government notices, pay required state fees, and verify that her "wealthy" customers are in fact sufficiently wealthy to meet the definition of "accredited investor." Prior to September 2013, Mary's method of seeking capital could have been perceived as a general solicitation or advertising—and therefore illegal—because anyone walking into her store could see the flyer, not just those persons that already knew her. When Title II of the Jumpstart Our Business Startups Act of 2012 was implemented by the SEC (new Regulation D Rule 506(c)) in September 2013, Mary's method of general solicitation became legal, provided she complies with Rule 506(c)'s investor accreditation proof requirements and accepts only accredited investors. To be compliant with existing law (Regulation D Rule 506(b)), she could communicate with existing customers if she knew them well enough to know whether they were sophisticated about business matters—but not before they are personally known to her. Mary can raise capital in the manner she was using the crowdfunding exemption under Title III (crowdfunding) (I use the term "investment crowdfunding" interchangeably with the SEC"s term "regulation crowdfunding" in this book), provided that her advertising is limited to directing investors to contact only her investor portal or licensed securities broker dealer that has been engaged to sell her securities. Also, she will be able to raise capital under Title IV (Regulation A), if she is conducting an offering in her state in compliance with Regulation A's requirements, which allow her to publicly offer and sell her securities, provided that her financial statements are annually audited, among other requirements. Hopefully, Mary seeks competent securities counsel before she makes a legal mistake that hurts her and her business.

So, it seems natural that there would be an assumption on the part of many people that if everyone is doing it, it must be legal. Of course, without following the requirements of each exemption from registration, general solicitation for investment capital is illegal. And although it's a numbers game of getting caught by regulators or getting sued by one's investors, the consequences of getting sued by a government financial regulator or of having in the public record a private investor's judgment for fraud against you can be destructive or fatal to one's business and personal reputation.

Here is what the risk of damage to reputation boils down to if you get cross-ways with the government. Assume that you are innocent in your mind of all wrongdoing. Consider the following circumstances and consequences and decide whether you can live with them:

- There are no rules or regulations governing when or if the SEC or a state securities commission will publish your name in connection with a suit they have filed against you.
- There are also no rules requiring government agencies to remove your name after a certain time period or remove or update your status publicly if you ultimately win against them.
- Your name will be on the world wide web forever, most likely associated with the word "fraud," and, in the financial services industry, every time you open a bank account, credit card account, brokerage account, or apply for a mortgage, you will probably get turned down because Know Your Customer rules requires financial institutions to routinely review the Office of Foreign Assets Control (OFAC) and World-Check databases in connection with account-opening transactions and for routine customer account surveillance.
- Your local news media may well have received a fax from the SEC or the state regulator that resulting in a story or two or three and the destruction of your local reputation.
- People that didn't like you before that get wind of the negative news may write articles or republish the news articles to make sure you are known for what you are in their minds—a crook.
- Your relationships with spouse and kids may well be strained. Weak marriages will probably fail.
- Financial stress in the home will be at an all-time high now that you need lawyers for your defense, unless of course the government has

frozen your bank and brokerage accounts and notified your mortgage company to make sure it is on top of you to accelerate the due date of your mortgage.

- Getting a new job in the community may well be impossible as your reputation becomes toxic.

Once you have bumped into the government system, your name never gets out of it, and you are more likely to be a target of regulators or criminal authorities in the future. If your name comes up again, you will be presumed guilty by government investigators and prosecutors and are likely to be vigorously investigated for the purpose of bringing an action against you. This is the reality. Can you live with reality?

"Why would the government worry about me? I'm too small," is exactly the wrong concept of one's exposure. The smaller you are, the less likely you are going to be able to fight back and win. It is a numbers game for the bureaucracy, too. It has budgetary restraints, but it always wants to win so it will always outspend you. It wants to bring more or less the same number of cases as in the previous year so it can justify its funding requests. The government bureaucracy has a better chance of guaranteeing its statistics and projections by pursuing small entities and entrepreneurs. In other words, the government bureaucracy often takes on those with the smallest war chests available to defend themselves. The smaller you are, the *bigger* target you are. The exception to this rule of thumb is that if you are a high profile person—someone in the media—you have a better than average chance of being used as a high profile example of what not to do.

Private securities plaintiffs are motivated differently. As a group they are motivated more by money and the possibility of wealth distribution at your expense than of punishing you—unless in their minds they are in a morally superior position and have the means by which to teach you a lesson.

All of this is longhand for saying that a prudent person should think hard about the risks of something going wrong in their offering, including the risks of bringing strangers into their companies and into their deals. The best time to think about these issues is *before* accepting their money.

Assuming that you are willing to move forward, let's start to plan a capital raise from the lawyer's perspective with a view to keeping you and your company out of trouble.

Chapter 2

TAKING INVENTORY

Your People, Your Cash Needs, and Your Friends

Limiting your litigation risk should start by taking inventory of your company's people, your cash needs, and your friends. What do I mean by this?

You need to perform a simple self-analysis to determine what type of private offering you are eligible to conduct. When you know those answers the direction of your planning can be focused. Starting first with the members of management and key employees, what are their backgrounds? I make the officers and directors of all of my corporate finance clients complete a background questionnaire. (A sample officer and director questionnaire is provided as a bonus for purchasing this book.) This lengthy document forces management to disclose to me their education history, work experience, ownership of securities, involvement in lawsuits, duties at the company, compensation, benefits, and involvement in related-party transactions, among other topics. Most of the questions are sensitive and are not the kinds of things that people bring up in casual conversation. I need to know the answers, and, unless the enterprise is entirely owned and managed by a single family, chances are that most or many of the responses to the questionnaires would be surprising to the others in the company. What we are looking for are background issues that we want to disclose to investors as material information before they make their investment decision. This is often a counter-intuitive process because I want you to tell me what you ordinarily would not tell me in casual conversation. Certainly there is some information issuers may not want to disclose because it might make it harder for the issuer to raise funds. These are precisely the same issues that, if they are not disclosed at the outset, may later become central to any subsequent dispute between the company and investor. This scenario arises repeatedly because the issuer may be staring at an investor who wants to throw cash at the company and is afraid of losing the opportunity. If the issuer lets greed or desperation control its rational thought process, then it may be setting itself up for a very ugly future in the court system.

Thoroughly knowing management's background is critical. Three of the exemptions from SEC securities offering registration contain "bad boy" disqualification provisions. If the issuer, its officers, directors, or significant shareholders or persons participating in the offering have been the subjects of criminal proceedings, government financial regulatory proceedings, or have been sanctioned by a non-government regulatory authority such as NYSE or FINRA, the issuer may well be precluded from utilizing a Regulation A, or Regulation D Rule 504 or Rule 506 private offering. Obviously, the issuer should want to know whether it is disqualified from certain types of offerings. Being disqualified from a Rule 506 offering in my view is a big deal because this is the offering that has no dollar limit and is not subject to concurrent state securities offering laws. It is the most-often utilized private offering exemption.

Another major deciding factor is how much cash you need. The federal offering exemptions have limits of $1,000,000 (Title III Crowdfunding)), $5,000,000 (Regulation D Rule 504), $50,000,000 (Title IV Regulation A), and No Dollar Limit (Regulation D Rule 506(b), 506(c), and Regulation S). Each exemption has specific limitations that must be complied with such as the number of unaccredited investors that can participate (which ranges from zero in a Regulation D Rule 506(c) offering to no limit in a Title III crowdfunding or Title IV Regulation A offering), the minimum information that must be disclosed to unaccredited investors, the knowledge and sophistication of unaccredited investors, the maximum amount of money that each investor can invest, the possible need to verify the accredited status of investors claiming to be accredited, and, in the case of offshore sales, the need to ensure no securities are sold back into the United States within a one-year period. Of course, there are pros and cons with each type of offering. One of the significant distinctions between offering types is that Rule 506, Regulation A,[3] and investment crowdfunding offerings preempt state securities registration requirements; thus, the states cannot assert their rules or review requirements as to the conduct of the offering. This aspect provides significant cost and time savings because compliance with each state's securities requirements is cumbersome, expensive, and time-consuming. Regulation A can be, and Rule 504 offerings are, subject to state offering regulations.

Along with these considerations is the question of what character of investor you are willing to accept. Strangers or friends? Wealthy or not so wealthy? If you are conducting a debt offering and have the ability to pay off the debt as agreed in the offering terms, the character of the investors in one sense may seem less important because you are going to get rid of them all with the last principal or interest payment. But don't be lax with your compliance with applicable exemption requirements because debt offerings all have the same exemptions from registration restrictions as equity offerings. The point here is that investors in a debt offering can still sue you, so you should investigate their characters before agreeing to accept their funds.

With equity offerings, once you let the investors in, unless you have a built-in redemption right where you can purchase their interests back in the future, you might be stuck with them indefinitely. Investors hate redemption rights. Issuers love them. You should know who these folks are and be sure that they can afford to be invested for the long haul. Some will have a public history of litigation. Try to avoid these toxic investors, if at all possible.

3 For a Regulation A offering to preempt state registration requirements, the offering must be limited to accredited investors.

In the publicly-advertised offerings (crowdfunding, Regulation D Rule 506(c), and Regulation A), anyone can show up and buy their way into your enterprise if you are not careful. Prudent entrepreneurs will let investors in their deals only if they are known to them. This policy is consistent with the SEC's longstanding policy that only friends, family, and pre-existing business relations can be communicated with to maintain the private nature of the Regulation D (Rules 504 and 506(b)) offering. Hopefully, your friends and family are wealthy and generous. Most entrepreneurs probably know only other starving entrepreneurs. This scenario led to the 2012 recession-driven legislation known as the Jumpstart Our Business Startups Act (JOBS Act) which reduced the SEC's and the states' control of private capital formation. Investment crowdfunding and advertised Rule 506 offerings are some of the hallmarks of this legislation. I caution you to consider the merits of advertised Rule 506 and investment crowdfunded offerings because you will be letting strangers into your company.[4]

Crowdfunding means different things to different people but in each category involves the solicitation of funds from strangers using the world wide web or social media as the primary means of solicitation. The JOBS Act's investment-style of crowdfunding will become legal once the SEC promulgates rules to implement it. This type of crowdfunding is also known as equity (or debt) crowdfunding and is distinguished from donor, pre-purchase, and rewards crowdfunding. Donor crowdfunding essentially is the solicitation for gifts or donations from strangers for personal use or charitable causes. Pre-purchase crowdfunding is the solicitation for pre-production donations in exchange for the promise that the donor will receive the produced product or a prototype of the company's product. Rewards crowdfunding is the solicitation for contributions to a project such as a film production where the donors are promised public recognition or a small role in the film. Thus, issuers and entrepreneurs can utilize the non-investment types of crowdfunding at the present time.

4 This is the case if you conducted a registered IPO as well. In an IPO, there is the possibility that a liquid market will develop that will enable investors to exit from your company and resell their investments publicly. This is not necessarily the same when a private offering is conducted. Investors in a private offering may have to wait indefinitely to realize a liquidity event. The company may never go public, or a secondary market for the company's securities may not develop, or the expected revenue from the pooled asset vehicle may not materialize. In these circumstances, a probable way out of the company or the investment vehicle will be for the investors to sue for relief.

Investment crowdfunding contains the limitation that issuers can solicit funds from potential investors nationwide, but the solicitations must direct prospective investors to a registered broker dealer or a registered "portal" where information about the offering can be learned. Issuers are not permitted to solicit and receive funds directly from investors.

Likewise, an advertised Rule 506(c) offering carries with it the limitation that the issuer must take reasonable steps to verify the accredited status of each investor. This type of offering will also carry with it the risk that if a single unaccredited investor invests, and the issuer lacks adequate documentation of the investor's qualifying assets or income, then the entire exemption may be void. In that case, the issuer and affiliated participants in the offering may be jointly and severally liable for the full amount of the proceeds raised.

What is the path? As a general matter, I favor use of Rule 506(b), the unadvertised unlimited offering exemption. There may be reasons that any particular client issuer would prefer another exemption, but Rule 506(b) and its preemptive ability over state law weigh heavily in my thinking. While in some states it can be simple to follow state law exemptions—or conduct a registered state offering—the offerings must still meet the federal exemption requirements. In addition, such offerings are limited to state residents. If someone from another state gets into the offering, this could be a problem for the issuer. Such concerns are largely avoided when using Rule 506(b). However, I am certain that many clients will want to advertise their private offering using the new exemptions, including Rule 506(c), because they may lack wealthy friends and family. For example, investor crowdfunding and Regulation A could be utilized to conduct an accredited-investor only offering, raising up to $1 million or $50 million respectively, while not having to worry about verifying an investor's accredited status as required by Rule 506(c). Investor crowdfunding and Regulation A do not require proof of accredited status. Why admit hundreds of unaccredited future class action plaintiffs into the company?

Chapter 3

Mindset of Management

Corporate Pirates or Kumbayah-Culture?

Setting the tone of corporate culture is one of management's important functions. Management's values are judged by evidence of its actions. What culture is communicated to employees and the outside world? The answer to this question may determine whether a company is situated to deflect investor complaints, regulatory investigations, and also criminal investigations. If it is the corporate culture to pay attention to its internal operations and how those operations may affect investors, the company is likely to have in place structural systems, i.e., internal controls. These would operate to safeguard assets and proprietary information, and would document and retain evidence of transactions and ensure that financial information of the company is accurately and timely provided to management and disseminated to investors. What are management's ethics? A culture of white lies or honoring hand-shake agreements? If the company is internally sound because it has implemented appropriate systems of internal control, the company may be in a better position to deflect typical investor allegations of breach of fiduciary duties and fraudulent activities by the company. A company that does not take steps to protect itself in the ordinary course of conducting business or whose management lacks integrity may not survive lawsuits asserting merely negligence-based state law theories of misrepresentation in the offer and sale of securities. Walking the talk is a first line of defense.

Small companies may well have a clean slate on which to write. Forethought given to building internal structure as companies plan to grow may distinguish them in intangible ways. For one aspect, they may exude an aura of professionalism in their communications with investors and the outside world. Building confidence in the investor ranks will tend to keep them pacified and less inclined to have their legal counsels inquire whether management carries officer and director insurance. This culture of management and the corporation's communications with investors are calculated and scrutinized to produce positive thoughts in the minds of investors, and, if the company is large enough, in the minds of securities analysts. There is no intention of deception in this culture, only the delivery of material, truthful information. A company that demonstrates a culture of legal compliance should avoid major liabilities resulting from its investor base. Where is this fictional company, you wonder? Comedian Rodney Dangerfield would say, "How about Fantasyland?"[5] Fictional or not, it is the intention to build and the commencement of building a defense of integrity that matters. The fantasy should be limited to the concept that systems can and will be implemented perfectly, while the reality is that you have systems in place, you tested them in reasonable real-world scenarios, and you determined that the systems are robust but, of course, not perfect.

Here is a statement from the SEC explaining why it *did not* sue a company that violated the federal securities laws:

> *The SEC has determined not to bring an enforcement action against First Solar due to the company's extraordinary cooperation with the investigation among several other factors. Prior to Polizzotto's selective disclosure on September 21, First Solar cultivated an environment of compliance through the use of a disclosure committee that focused on compliance with Regulation FD. The*

5 "Back to School" scene available at http://www.youtube.com/watch?v=YlVDGmjz7eM

> *company immediately discovered Polizzotto's selective disclosure and promptly issued a press release the next morning before the market opened. First Solar then quickly self-reported the misconduct to the SEC. Concurrent with the SEC's investigation, First Solar undertook remedial measures to address the improper conduct. For example, the company conducted additional Regulation FD training for employees responsible for public disclosure.*[6]

Statements like this from the federal government are almost as rare as a sighting of Halley's Comet. This situation dealt not with a capital raising transaction but with a public company's reporting of bad news to the marketplace. My point here is that the culture established by management can make or break the enterprise in times when the government is at the door. Most companies that suffer through a securities investigation spend thousands or hundreds of thousands of dollars on legal fees and still get sued or indicted. Most companies do not recover from this type of wringing.

The goal here is to do something that is proactive before problems are encountered. Every effort helps, but the effort must be continuous and genuine. Looking at the worst case scenario, you as the defendant in a criminal securities trial, imagine facing an allegation that if you didn't know what was going on at the company, you were willfully blind (to the obvious fact that there was a pink elephant standing in the room) and should be convicted ... of securities fraud or some related type of financial crime like intentional records destruction or conspiracy to commit securities fraud. You need to offer credible testimony in your defense, probably from other witnesses, that there was a structure in place that was reasonable, that was tested, and worked and that there was no intention to mismanage, deceive investors, or destroy records with criminal intent. Therefore, you can argue that the government's viewpoint is based upon incomplete data, should be rejected, and you should be acquitted. While simplistic, in my experience, innocent people do get tried for crimes they did not commit, and their ability to walk out the front door of the courthouse or be wrongly convicted may boil down to circumstantial evidence of their lack of intent to do wrong.

---

6 Securities and Exchange Commission, http://www.sec.gov/News/PressRelease/Detail/PressRelease/1370539799034#.UjEfj53D_IV (last visited Sep. 11, 2013).

Jumping to the first contact with prospective investors, what can be done to limit litigation risk? First of all, don't promise anything except that you will provide the prospect with a written disclosure document and subscription agreement. The plaintiff's way around your documentation of the transaction is the claim that he was fraudulently or negligently induced to enter the transaction. Although your written documents will deny that, such allegations in a civil action typically survive initial motions to dismiss the complaint and must be weeded out through discovery. The problem is that ultimately such claims are he said/she said claims, often with no other witnesses. They might make it to trial, and corporate defendants who cannot demonstrate that they walk on water are probably going to lose at trial. Juries want to believe the little guy, and unless he can be shown to be untruthful, which is often difficult, such allegations are better off quietly settled. If possible, all oral communications with investors should be witnessed and recorded if state law allows and the parties consent to recording.

Going back to my micro-finance networking event example in the Introduction, I watched start-up companies give ten-minute presentations and ask for money from a crowd of people that I do not think they knew beforehand. I do not think anything was recorded, and no one passed out any documents of any kind. These were pure oral solicitations supported by PowerPoint presentations. One presenter didn't know how much money his company wanted and threw around a range of numbers. Prospective investors asked some good questions, but I was not tempted to throw a penny at these folks. Why would I write a check to anyone who presents no internal control structure that would stop these folks from accepting my check, paying themselves a salary that was roughly the same amount as my investment, and then taking an extended or permanent vacation to a remote island paradise? I think that the presence of an effective system of internal control, one that has at least some meaningful checks and balances in place to prevent theft or misappropriation, is a great marketing message to potential investors.

Of course, I am speculating as to the bona fides of the promoters that I observed. They may have been great people, had the best intentions, and would have used my funds appropriately had I invested. But how can I, a potential investor in this context, know anything about anybody on a first meeting? However, in my view, use of investor proceeds to pay management's salary is not a corporate purpose, unless the investor has knowingly consented. In my view, company *revenues* are not supposed to support payroll expenses, unless the investor is aware that investment funds are being used to support payroll expenses. Absent a disclosure of the intended use of investment funds, an investor's funds are capital finance contributions and should be used as such whether or not the offering documents specifically limit usage to a particular purpose. I say this because many times I have seen private offering documents that are silent or vague as to the proposed use of proceeds, and sometimes this is deliberate. I understand that management may be protected to an extent by the "business judgment rule," a common law defense that shields management's decision-making from charges of negligent operation of a business. What I am talking about is the integrity of management. If I wanted to buy the company president a Ferrari, I would give it to him directly on his birthday. As an investor, I want my investment money being used to grow and expand the business. To me, integrity of management is doing the right thing even when no document exactly prohibits you from giving yourself a corporate gift funded by investor money and no one is looking over your shoulder. A little dodge here, a little corner-cut there. A white lie to pacify someone here. It all adds up over time, and something bad should be expected to happen to management and the company to correct the imbalance in the universe. The investors cannot be blamed for suing when they learn of the high lifestyle management is living when revenues are not increasing. Management can easily avoid such accusations by doing what it knows is the right thing to do.

Alas, I digress. If we start with the company's written materials delivered to prospective investors, what should they contain?

First of all, you should consider that the founders of a company can be investors in need of a disclosure document. You may have a small LLC (limited liability company) with three members. Perhaps one or all of them are contributing funding. It might be prudent to prepare an offering disclosure document (known as a private placement memorandum or private offering memorandum) for each of them to set a ground floor as to what was known about the investment objectives and risks of investment. This may serve the wealthier of the three members because if something goes wrong—even if all three are accredited investors—the less wealthy might take action against the deepest pocket in the group. One never knows.

Second, whether you are forming or investing in a partnership, LLC, or small company, do not let the informality of humble and friendly beginnings lull you into failing to insist that all shareholders or members or partners execute an agreement that sets forth how shareholders or partners can be bought out, when they can force their exit, and what happens to the partner's share and what are the survivor's rights upon the death or disability of a partner. Procedures for valuation of equity interests, voting deadlock, forced and voluntary sale, rights of survivors to vote shares, and anything else that may be pertinent can and should be negotiated at the outset of the enterprise. Once the enterprise gets going, everybody will be too busy to consider these issues and will feel uncomfortable bringing them up. However, people's lifestyles change as they mature, their cash needs change, and one may want to get out at an inopportune time. Plan for this "corporate divorce" with a "corporate prenuptial" agreement. It will save everyone a large headache in the future and will help keep friends from becoming enemies.

Third, structure the articles of incorporation and bylaws to provide for maximum indemnification under state law for all officers, directors, and agents of the company. This incentivizes management to remain friendly and not sue each other because the sued party will be able to make the company pay for her defense. Likewise, shareholders will be disincentivized to sue the company if doing so will cause the company to be bankrupted through the mandatory reimbursement of legal defense costs.

Fourth, consider putting in a mandatory arbitration clause for all disputes between the company and its officers and directors. That clause may help keep the company's dirty laundry out of the court system and out of public view.

Fifth, include a redemption rights provision in the articles of incorporation and consider putting a procedure for valuation of private company shares in the bylaws. If one day the issuer needs to get rid of a hostile shareholder and can afford to buy out that class of equity, it has the organic right to do so.

These are some ideas. There is much that can be done to establish the rights of the parties to the corporation. The above list may help you to be creative with this process and hopefully prevent costly litigation. Hopefully, you will seek competent legal counsel to counsel you on the wisdom of your creative ideas.

The deal documents are where the company should not skimp on legal fees. While attorneys also search the internet and other sources for template documents upon which to base a pleading or contract or disclosure document or whatever, you risk being reckless in using documents used in other deals, including downloadable documents, unless you are appropriately trained or supervised. While it is true that there is much boilerplate legalese that appears in many documents, you need to know why it is there and when it needs to be modified or supplemented. The document you locate on the world wide web will not tell you what you are missing or why a provision was drafted a certain way. There is no user manual out there, and some boilerplate provisions are state-specific or may have tax consequences. Play lawyer at your own risk, not your company's.

Back to investors. The company needs to formally authorize any attempt to raise capital. That is addressed in a board resolution or majority shareholder consent. As I mentioned before, you want to document every representation made to any investor so they can't sue successfully—or will not think of suing—for fraudulent or negligent inducement to contract. So-called "big boys" may not insist and may not want the issuer to prepare any disclosure document for them, and that may be fine so long as the issuer knows these accredited investors well. The purpose of preparing a disclosure document is to protect the issuer from subsequent claims of false or materially misleading disclosure or non-disclosure. Protect the company with a thoroughly drafted private offering memorandum and deliver it to the prospective investor before their check or wire transfer is accepted as payment.

All investments should be accomplished with a purchase and sale agreement or securities subscription agreement. Some prefer a subscription agreement because it suggests that the acceptance of the investor's purchase is conditional by the company. A properly drafted securities purchase agreement provides that acceptance is subject to approval by the company, so in practical effect I have not noticed any difference. There are many topics that such documents should include. Among them are the investor's representation of how they qualify as being accredited. Even if the investor is not accredited, his representation in writing that he was accredited at the time of the securities transaction will usually bind him if he later sues. Courts enforce contracts, and the representations made by the parties in writing are hard to back out of. Some states have warning notices that must be given to investors advising them that they have a cooling off period before they can be bound by the investment agreement. I put a notice right on the securities purchase agreement so no investor can come back and claim that they didn't receive the notice. This often can be very important because the failure to demonstrate that the notice under state law was delivered means that the investor has an automatic right of rescission until the notice is provided. Because of a failure to deliver a state notice, the investor may be able to greatly expand the generally short statutes of limitation that apply to securities offerings. The statute of limitations is the issuer's friend, and anything that can be done to accelerate its bar date I advocate to clients. This is why fraudulent and negligent inducement to contract claims (and negligence-based claims) are a problem for issuers. Statutes of limitation often do not run on tort claims until the fraudulent or negligent representation was discovered, or the negligence should have been discovered, whenever that date may be. It usually is not the date that the transaction occurred. Breach of (investment) contract claims operate differently. Statutes of limitations periods on contract claims typically commence on the date that the parties executed the contract at issue. If no written agreements or contracts or disclosure documents have been delivered to or executed by the investor, you have little or no ability to rely on a statute of limitations defense.

Delivery of the state notice technically does not apply to Rule 506 offerings because state notice delivery is a condition on an offering that is preempted by federal law. However, some courts hold that the right to the federal exemption has to be affirmatively established, so in those jurisdictions it is probably safe to rely on the "notice delivery" defense. Most plaintiff's attorneys probably will not know of this nuance if you argue that the statute of limitations has run based upon early delivery of the notice in a Rule 506 offering. I typically embed deal documents with state disclosures in case for some reason later on the transaction is disqualified from use of Rule 506. Then there is the possibility that the transaction will continue to have certain defenses available to protect the issuer.

The so-called "bespeaks caution" defense (the "we warned you" defense) is one that every issuer can use, but it hinges on whether a written disclosure document was delivered to the prospective investor at or before the time the investor wrote her check to the issuer. Presumably, if the investor received the warnings in writing of the material risks of the offering and of the company, the investor cannot be heard to complain in court that she didn't know the risks. This doctrine operates as a safe harbor for claims of fraud by investors if they were adequately warned in writing. This defense is established with a thoroughly written disclosure document that was provided to the investor on or before the time that they invested.

The defense of "good faith" is available under federal law to negate charges of intentional or recklessly fraudulent activity. The evidence of good faith can be in the form of circumstantial evidence, testimony from witnesses, or documents. Whichever way it can be proven, the fact that attention was paid to establishing systems in a corporation that were robust and effective, even if they were defeated in the context being litigated, can go a long way to rebut fraud charges.

The ultimate defenses are that the plaintiff cannot establish his facts, or, even if he can establish them, his facts fail to establish a claim upon which relief can be granted.

The takeaway points are that management's mindset and the culture of legal compliance it fosters—or not—determines the extent to which companies will take the high road with their investors. I see this as a first line of defense for lawsuit prevention. Some companies view their investors as being greedy vipers deserving of being stepped on. Such companies, I believe, will waste much time, money, and energy in needless litigation. Other companies view investors the way the securities laws view them—as needing protection. A company that tries to protect its investors protects itself to an extent by preempting or pacifying their potential to drag the company to the courthouse. Legal compliance is not free, but companies can take simple but meaningful steps to protect themselves in transactions with investors and in ongoing corporate communications. The "ounce of prevention" strategy should help the company promote its business as a safer investment for such reason and thereby reduce the overall risk of litigation.

Chapter 4

What Does "General Solicitation and Advertising" Mean

and Why Is It a Problem?

Prior to enactment of the JOBS Act of 2012, Regulation D under the federal securities laws prohibited general solicitation and advertising in connection with private investment offerings. The basic idea is that registered public offerings are examined by the SEC for compliance with disclosure requirements. These registered securities transactions can then be offered and sold to the general public. Private offerings, on the other hand, are not reviewed by the SEC; therefore, there is greater risk that disclosures will be inadequate for certain types of investors, especially if the amount of persons solicited to invest is numerous or the cash sought to be raised exceeds $1,000,000. As defined by Regulation D Rule 502(c), general solicitation or general advertising includes, among other things, "(1) [a]ny advertisement, article, notice or other communication published in any newspaper, magazine, or similar media," and "(2) [a]ny seminar or meeting whose attendees have been invited by any general solicitation or general advertising."

Title II of the JOBS Act directed the SEC to amend Rule 506 of Regulation D to release the ban on general solicitation and advertising provided that only accredited investors were permitted to invest in the advertised offering. Title III of the JOBS Act (crowdfunding) contains a similar concept. Title III permits a maximum capital raise of $1,000,000, but any number of investors with any degree of knowledge of business can invest. In this respect crowdfunding is similar to Rule 504 in that there is no limit to the number of unaccredited investors that may participate in the offering, but the dollar amount is limited to $5,000,000. Instead, Title II imposes restrictions on how much money investors can invest based upon a scale of net worth and income.

The big news, though, is that general solicitation and advertising of capital raises is legal for Rule 506(c), crowdfunding and Regulation A offerings. Meanwhile, issuers may continue to use the old rules (Regulation D Rules 506(b) and 504) indefinitely if they will comply with the ban on general solicitation and advertising associated with these rules.

Here are some examples of what the SEC has said you cannot do under the *old* rules, which are still in effect:

- Send accredited investor questionnaires to the top 3% of your customer database of 250,000 customers (7,500 questionnaires);
- Send investment and business information to a list of licensed professionals;
- Publish a tombstone-style announcement that you have completed a private securities offering if you are likely to conduct another offering or one is ongoing; or
- While, or in anticipation of, conducting a private offering, mail a brochure describing an investment opportunity to members of an industry association or trade group; distribute brochures at a public event, or advertise in a trade journal.

Since advertising and general solicitation connotes a lack of pre-existing relationship and a generalized form of communication, the issuer may be able to hold a meeting with a small number of prospective investors provided that the issuer can demonstrate that it did not create the invitation list from a generic source such as a list of attorneys licensed in a particular jurisdiction. The SEC advises that "[t]he types of relationships with offerees that may be important in establishing that a general solicitation has not taken place are those that would enable the issuer (or a person acting on its behalf) to be aware of the financial circumstances or sophistication of the persons with whom the relationship exists or that otherwise are of some substance and duration." A permissible example of this is where a securities broker dealer sends out 50 questionnaires per month to local businessmen and professionals using lists created by the sender where the proposed solicitation is generic in nature, and does not reference a specific securities investment offered or contemplated to be offered, and a procedure is in place to ensure that no one who receives a mailing is able to invest in a security that was being offered while at the time of the mailing. The business relationship is substantiated with responding persons for a period of at least 45 days before any of them are provided materials concerning a particular investment.

Thus, a substantive relationship may be established with a person who has provided a satisfactory response to a questionnaire that enables the sender to have sufficient information to evaluate the prospective offeree's sophistication and financial circumstances.

Engaging in general solicitation and advertising violates the "private" nature of private securities offerings. Unless such securities offerings are registered or are offered in compliance with new rules promulgated by the SEC pursuant to the requirements of the JOBS Act, such offerings will violate the federal and possibly state securities laws.

Chapter 5

Penalties and Problem Areas

The solicitation of investment funds is highly regulated at both the state and federal level. Federal law requires that every *offer* of an investment opportunity must be registered with the U.S. Securities and Exchange Commission, unless an exemption from registration applies (meaning that you can legally conduct an unregistered securities offering).

Thus, in practical effect, there are ways to structure a proposed investment solicitation so that the offer is exempt from registration under federal law and state law. Even if structured properly, the company's execution of the offer must be compliant with the antifraud provisions of federal law and the antifraud laws of each applicable state. Antifraud statutes and regulations make it illegal to commit fraud in the offer, purchase, or sale of a security.

Noncompliance with applicable registration and/or antifraud laws and regulations can result in lengthy imprisonment and fines. Most, if not all, federal and state securities laws are punishable both civilly and criminally. Investors under most state laws have a right of rescission (meaning that the purchaser can cancel the purchase and get a full refund) or a right to rescissionary damages (meaning that if the issuer cannot return all of the investment purchase money, the issuer and other liable persons will owe a debt to the purchaser) for an issuer's non-compliance with registration or antifraud requirements. And in some states, the officers and directors of the issuer must register as "brokers" before they can solicit investments in these states.

Unregistered Securities Sales

The offering of an unregistered security made in reckless disregard for a regulatory requirement—such as a registration requirement—is a felony at both the federal and state level, and the seller has the burden of establishing as a matter of law that it complied with at least one applicable exemption from registration.

For government civil prosecutions of unregistered securities sales, the seller is *strictly* liable for the failure to register, and the seller has the burden of establishing as a matter of law that it complied with at least one applicable exemption from registration. Demonstrating compliance with an exemption statute *after* one has been sued for failing to register usually is not a successful defense strategy. This is because the government typically will have investigated and concluded that no exemption from registration applied to the offering, and it will be prepared to demonstrate that any evidence that you can muster in your defense will not be sufficient to prove your entitlement to an exemption. In addition, the prosecution will educate the court that a tie in the battle of proof should not result in victory for the defendant. The government will argue that the better policy is to favor a scheme of registration and full disclosure than to reward issuers who take the unregistered route of presumptively inadequate and governmentally unscrutinized disclosure. This is not to say that you cannot claim an exemption. It is to say that that you have to demonstrate your compliance with the exemption. Remember also that the regulatory scheme mandates registration of all offerings and permits exemptions from registration only if the requirements of the exemption have been complied with.

Let me demonstrate from a litigation lawyer's viewpoint how simple it is for an investor-plaintiff to allege and prove a claim for unregistered securities sales. A plaintiff need only allege and prove these facts:

1. No securities registration statement was in effect for the offering purchased by the plaintiff;
2. The defendant sold the securities purchased by plaintiff; and
3. For a federal action, but not required for a state unregistered securities claim, the defendant used the means and instrumentalities of interstate transportation or communication in connection with the sale or offer to sell.

These allegations are simple to prove. Obtaining an affidavit from a state securities commission or from the SEC stating that no registration statement was in effect for the issuer during the relevant time period of the offering is all that is required to prove the first requirement. These affidavits are obtainable with a telephone call or a letter and payment of a fee of a few dollars.

The defendant typically will be the issuer of the securities but may also be the officers and directors and any sales-persons involved in selling the securities to the plaintiff. Proof of who the participants were typically is not challenged by those who dealt directly with the plaintiff or by the issuer. That forecloses the second required element. If the case is brought by a state securities commission or the SEC, the government does not have to prove that there were any purchasers. All that is required by statute is proof that an offering was conducted. If the issuer advertised the offering, a sample of the advertisement or the testimony of one investor could be offered as evidence. Very simple.

The last element is only required in federal cases. Unless the offer was communicated orally, which is rare, almost certainly the internet, the phones, or the mails or common carrier were used to communicate some aspect of purchase or sale information. This requirement is rarely challenged.

For a private plaintiff to be victorious, he must also prove his monetary damages, which can established with a copy of his check used to make the investment and his testimony that he never sold, cannot sell, or sold before a significant price rise, to show the change (loss) in investment value. Regulators need only prove that the unregistered offering occurred and can be victorious merely by obtaining a court determination that a defendant violated the registration requirements without showing anyone was unjustly enriched.

Upon proof of these requirements, a defendant must then prove that the offering qualified for an exemption from registration or that an individual defendant was not a necessary participant in the offering. (The scope of this book is aimed at reducing litigation risk for the corporate issuer and its management. Thus, this book is concerned primarily with the exemptions from registration available to securities issuers and not with defenses available to individual persons. My law firm, of course, also represents individuals.)

For a violation of the registration provisions, whether in civil or criminal cases, the only defense is proof of compliance with an available exemption from registration. The penalties in a SEC case for unregistered securities sales typically involve more than just fines. The remedy is usually also injunctive in nature and includes an injunction from future securities law violations, a mandatory accounting of all funds raised, an order requiring disgorgement of all funds raised, and prejudgment interest at the Internal Revenue Service's underpayment of tax rate. Civil money penalties are awarded based upon guidance given in the form of a statute that breaks down misconduct into fines based upon the number of injured investors, whether fraud was involved, and whether regulatory requirements were disregarded.

Here is an example of the risk of non-compliance:

> *A Connecticut court convicted Constance Andresen (her real name) of five counts of selling unregistered securities, although she was acquitted of five counts of securities fraud. The defendant claimed in her defense, among other arguments on appeal, that she relied on the advice of her lawyer in selling the unregistered securities. Approximately ninety people invested $1.3 million in her company that purportedly had a FDA-approved cancer-diagnosing device. The court noted that the corporation spent only $35,000 on research and development of the device and that the device was of little use in diagnosing cancer. Constance and her husband received approximately $1 million of the*

$1.3 million raised. She was sentenced to ten years in prison, suspended after two years, five years of probation, and a $10,000 fine.

Here the client blamed her lawyer as her defense against the state's accusation of selling unregistered securities. Reliance on legal counsel, the court held, was not a defense to the strict-liability crime of selling unregistered securities. Strict liability means, in essence, that if you committed the prohibited act (in this case, selling securities without filing a registration statement for them) whether or not you intended to do wrong, you are liable. The permissible defense is that the defendant's activities qualified for an exemption from registration; i.e., sufficient evidence by the defense must be put forth to show that an exemption such as the maximum dollar amount or the maximum number of offerees was not exceeded. This court made clear that in Connecticut, as in most jurisdictions, the defendant has the burden to prove entitlement to an exemption from registration and that the prosecutor does not have to disprove entitlement to any exemption to sustain a conviction. In other words, it is constitutionally permissible in this type of crime to require the defendant to offer evidence of innocence to prevent a conviction.

Lawyer or no lawyer, selling unregistered securities without taking the steps to qualify the offering under an exemption from registration can seriously affect the quality of your life and the extent of your property and your liberty.

Negligent or Fraudulent Misrepresentations

In most states, in criminal prosecutions, a negligent misrepresentation made in connection with the offer or sale of an investment is also punishable as a felony. A negligent misrepresentation is one meant to induce the buyer to accept the offer but which is based on material facts that the seller should have known were not true. A negligent misrepresentation of a material fact in an offer of securities is punishable as a felony in almost every state.

The only defense is that the issuer did not make false statements. There is no "good faith" defense. At the federal level and in certain states, in a civil case the government or the investor has a higher standard of proof—that the issuer was at least reckless in its representations made in connection with its offered investments. Good faith of the issuer applies only as a defense to a claim that the issuer knowingly or recklessly violated the fraud provisions. The defendant's good faith is not a defense to a claim of negligent misrepresentation.

A violation of antifraud provisions of the federal securities laws can carry a twenty or twenty-five-year sentence since the Sarbanes-Oxley Act was enacted, and a federal conspiracy charge carries a five-year sentence. If securities fraud seems a little too difficult to prove, prosecutors routinely charge mail or wire fraud on the same fact pattern and get the same twenty-year jail threat against a potential defendant.

In government civil securities actions, the penalties and remedies are usually the same whether the government established a violation of the antifraud provisions or the registration provisions. Every defendant is likely to be required to "disgorge" all purportedly ill-gotten gain, pay a civil fine plus pre-judgment interest at the IRS underpayment rate, and receive an injunction against securities registration and fraud violations in the future. If fraud is charged, small company executives may also be subject to a bar from serving a public company as an officer or director. Small company executives and entrepreneurs, whether involved in public reporting companies or privately-held enterprises, are likely also to receive a bar from participating in offerings of penny stock. What is penny stock? It is stock offered for less than five dollars per share, or is stock issued by a company that has net tangible assets of less than $5,000,000, or has average revenues of less than $6,000,000 in the last three-year period. The asset-based qualification depends on how many years the company has been in operation, while the revenue-based qualification requires sustained revenues for three years. Consider that most small company equity offerings are offered for less than five dollars per share and even fewer issuers have net tangible assets (i.e., total assets less intangible assets and liabilities) in excess of $2,000,000 (if the issuer has been in continuous operation for at least three years), or $5,000,000 (if the issuer has been in continuous operation for less than three years); or average revenue of at least $6,000,000 for the last three years. A company that does not meet these standards is a penny stock issuer if it issues equity or debt that is convertible into equity. Thus, most issuers and their equity-offering participants are at risk of being barred for life from raising capital if a federal securities regulatory action is brought against them.

Here is an example of what not to do, taken from a reported appellate decision from an Illinois court:

> *Emanuel Khan raised $1,465,200 from more than 35 people. He failed to register the stocks issued, or himself, as an agent as he was required to do under Illinois law. He also failed to inform prospective investors that he had a history of administrative and judicial securities proceedings brought against him. The court noted that for a three-year period money was raised from investors but that his company's total gross sales were only $2,429. However, Khan paid himself $489,545 for his services to the issuer. Khan was convicted of selling unregistered securities, securities fraud, corrupt business influence, and failing to register as a securities sales agent. He was sentenced to ten years in prison.*

No mention was made in the opinion whether Khan had told the investors that he would use nearly thirty percent of the total funds received to pay himself a salary. (To his credit, he only paid himself eleven percent of the gross proceeds per year, so maybe he didn't set out to burn 33% of the proceeds on his salary.) Presumably, he did not tell the investors about his compensation expectations, and the investors must have been upset about that. This is what "use of proceeds" is all about and why I highlight it below in this chapter. The opinion did not mention whether the balance of investors' funds was saved or spent on legitimate business expenses.

Other take-a-ways from this case: the court did not believe that it was okay for Mr. Khan, the entrepreneur, to receive approximately $1.5 million, spend a significant chunk on his compensation, and generate only token revenues. Legitimate start-up companies may never generate revenues. However, this is how the court system often operates when business people are dragged into it. People with no or little business experience, such as typical government investigators, lawyers, judges, and juries, parse out select facts and hold them under a microscope and pass judgments against entrepreneurs and business executives. That is our system. The safest place for business people to be is away from this system. Minimizing litigation risk while raising capital is serious business. There are few "business-oriented" or "commercial" courts in the country, but there are lots of retired or unemployed people able to serve on juries and who may have an axe to grind against corporate America. To top this off, the laws in every state favor the investor over the capital raiser.

Start-up companies take note: if you have raised capital from investors, there is no grace period for failing to execute your business plan. Investors who don't profit soon will complain, will sue, and may bring you down to a place you cannot get up from.

Lazy executives take note: the beauty of other people's money is not that it is inexpensive or that you didn't have to work for it. It is that the people who are providing it to you probably worked hard to get it, and though they are certainly motivated by their greed in expecting you to grow it further for them, they expect you to work at least as hard as they did to get the money in the first place. Expecting them to walk away when the investment goes sour on your watch is not a prudent business plan in the long run. They may come after you.

Serially lazy and wannabe executives take note: People in the finance business are heavily regulated. Some people get criminally prosecuted on their first run-in with the law. Others seem to be charmed and to get away with a lot. For the lucky ones, this generates a false sense of security in their minds. It also teaches them—and the marketplace around them—poor lessons about what is legally permissible. Clear, natural, common sense notions of right and wrong are not evident oftentimes in the regulated world of finance. It is a world of rules and exceptions. Both financiers and professionals get lulled into believing that their business practices or their interpretations of rules and statutes are correct because no one they know has gotten into trouble. Life steams onward until the government steps in to repaint the lines between black, gray, and white and imprint its view permanently on the lives of those caught in the wrong place at the wrong time. Many people stumble head-long and face-first into the regulated world of finance only to learn the hard way that it is not child's play.

Typical Problem Areas in Small Company Capital Raising Transactions

There are typical problem areas in small company offering documents that regulators and some plaintiff's attorneys will target for easy proof of a securities violation to frame their complaint against a securities issuer or its management. Some of these problem areas are: the completeness of the disclosure of the experience and track record of the issuers' management; disclosure of criminal and regulatory histories, disclosure of management's poor track record with prior companies they managed, lack of relevant SEC filings, failure to disclose negative news about the company or one of its products, lack of reasonable basis for financial projections, and intentional or deliberate misstating of financial results. The following additional categories deserve special mention.

Press Releases

Press releases are a lifeline to a company's connection with the investing public, and can be an economical means of spreading the corporate story. For public companies, without a steady flow of news, investor interest in even a large company will wane. There will be more sellers than buyers of the company's stock, and the company's stock price will decline. The SEC wants issuers to make a fair and balanced presentation of company news, as well as the disclosure of good and bad news. Many times, however, it is the company's press releases that are the vehicle through which misinformation is disseminated, through which stock prices are manipulated, and through which pump-and-dump schemes are perpetrated. Such schemes are most often associated with the over-the-counter stock market, but false press releases, most often misstated earnings releases, are associated with the larger publicly-owned companies. But there is no reason why false news should be limited to publicly-owned companies. Private companies, particularly when they are placed for sale or when raising capital, may have a financial incentive to make their image rosier.

Because press releases are necessarily brief in nature, an incomplete or overbroad statement made in a press release about the company or its product, even if drafted with innocent intentions, is relatively easy to do accidentally and can expose everyone participating in drafting the release as well to liability.

Principals, Promoters, Control Persons, and Related Parties

Principals, promoters, control persons, and parties related to the company are often the people that prospective investors should want to know the most about.

These individuals can be the unseen "man behind the curtain" in nefarious circumstances, or they can be the unintentionally omitted individual who exercises significant control over corporate policies, or who stands to benefit from a healthy opportunity to engage in business with the company while a spouse or other close relative is a key employee of the company. Thus, the regulations pertaining to disclosure in federal registered securities offerings place much emphasis on the complete disclosure of the backgrounds of these influential individuals. Deliberate or intentional non-disclosure of the identities of control persons, promoters, and related parties may serve to defeat the requirement of transparency to investors. Federal regulations require management and control persons to disclose a ten-year employment history with start and stop dates, explanations of periods of unemployment, and the disclosure of relevant criminal, regulatory, or financial litigation history in the preceding five years, unless a longer period of time is reasonable under the circumstances. In addition, individuals in management that presided over an insolvent business in the preceding ten-years have a disclosure requirement.

Disclosed and Actual Use of Proceeds

Telling investors in writing how you are going to use their investment funds may seem obvious, but many offering documents provide little or no disclosure how management of a company will use the proceeds from securities sales. When there is little disclosure in this area, corporate management may believe that it has discretionary use of the funds to pay their salaries, buy them gifts, or fund the entertainment account. Disclosure is required, as is follow-up reporting of how the proceeds were actually used, in a federal registration statement. In an unregistered offering, only savvy investors may notice the lack of specificity and demand guarantees as to the acceptable use of funds.

Intangible Assets

Many small dot.com or start-up companies tout their only asset: a patent or some form of intellectual property. The asset could also be a guarantee of some type or even a claim of insurance benefits. Companies valuing themselves highly based upon their intangible assets while seeking capital are classic red flags for regulators and investors. Conservative accountants may choose not to accept any value for intangible assets, especially if the assets are non-performing.

Celebrity Directors and Advisors

Borrowing the good name of someone famous may seem like an inexpensive marketing idea, but sometimes the famous person has never consented to the use of his or her name in conjunction with the company. While an association with a celebrity director or advisor may very well be legitimate, care should be taken on behalf of investors to ensure that the limits of the relationship are accurately disclosed.

Multiple Offerings

The risks of conducting multiple offerings include the possibility that exemptions from registration will be violated. For example, if a cap on fundraising is not monitored and adhered to, the cap may be exceeded and the ability to claim the exemption could be lost. Multiple Regulation D private placement offers, such as a debt offering and a simultaneous convertible debenture offering, will have to be consolidated if they seem to have a common purpose (such as financing acquisitions of contiguous real estate parcels) beyond the obvious point that they will each be used to fund the same company. Consolidation may mean that offering caps on particular offering exemptions have been exceeded or that qualifications such as an investors' sophistication or their unaccredited status which may not be a requirement in a smaller offering category are violations in a larger offering. Another example is when multiple offerings are conducted less than six months apart. If these offerings are part of a common plan of financing, have approximately the same offering price and other material terms, they probably have to be consolidated. If in doing so the cap of 35 non-accredited investors has been exceeded, or the dollar cap on a Rule 504 offering has been exceeded, the offering is in danger of being deemed an unregistered public offering.

Chapter 6

The Solicitation to the Investor

Making an Offer

What Is an Offer?

Each state has its own definition of "offer" but most will resemble the federal definition. Essentially, any communication of an investment opportunity is an "offer." Typically, an offer is a traditional oral or written communication of terms for sale of an investment opportunity. Such an offer may be well documented and detailed in the form of a written prospectus or private placement memorandum. However, the securities laws are designed to be interpreted liberally by the courts in order to encompass *all conduct* that touches upon a securities transaction, ensuring that all such conduct will be subject to government regulation. Because of its wide scope, even extremely vague statements or actions can be deemed to be offers. For example, an offer can include conduct designed to create broker interest in the type of business activity soon to be conducted by a company that will be making an offering of securities, even if the company's name was not mentioned in the communication. *Gearhart & Otis, Inc.*, 42 S.E.C. 1 (1964), *aff'd*, 348 F.2d 798 (D.C. Cir. 1965). The invitation to an investment planning seminar has been viewed by the SEC as an offer of a security. Vague offers or activities deemed to constitute an offer almost always run afoul of the securities laws, which require all offers to disclose all material facts.

An offer of what? An investment opportunity for federal securities laws purposes is defined as:

> "any note, stock, treasury stock, security future, security-based swap, bond, debenture, evidence of indebtedness, certificate of interest or participation, in any profit-sharing agreement, collateral-trust certificate, preorganization certificate or subscription, transferable share, investment contract, voting-trust certificate, certificate of deposit for a security, fractional undivided interest in oil, gas, or other mineral rights, any put, call, straddle, option, or privilege on any security, certificate of deposit, or group or index of securities (including any interest therein or based on the value thereof), or any put, call, straddle, option, or privilege entered into on a national securities exchange relating to foreign currency, or, in general, any interest or instrument commonly known as a "security", or any certificate of interest or participation in, temporary or interim certificate for, receipt for, guarantee of, or warrant or right to subscribe to or purchase, any of the foregoing." Securities Act of 1933, Section 2(a)(1).

Of all of the definitions of a "security" in the above statute, perhaps the most subtle and potentially devastating to the unwary entrepreneur is that of the "investment contract."

Here is an actual example of what can be at stake for offers of non-traditional investment opportunities, *i.e.*, those that are encompassed by the definition of an "investment contract":

A prospective condominium buyer contacted a real estate agent in another state seeking assistance with purchasing a condominium unit. The agent located a condo unit, and the investor purchased the unit from its owners who previously had purchased the unit from the condominium developer. Prior to the closing of the purchase and sale transaction, the buyer's real estate agent advised her client that he is eligible to participate in a rental pool created by the condominium developer whereby absentee owners could place their units up for rental and share in the net profits generated by units participating in the rental pool. Participation in the rental pool was optional. The seller of the condo was not a rental pool participant. Also, a property management company offered rental management contracts to unit owners. The buyer subsequently opted into the rental pool and entered into the property management contract. Apparently, the buyer became unhappy with his "investment." The buyer sued his real estate agent, claiming that she violated the antifraud provisions of the Securities Exchange Act of 1934 and SEC Rule 10b-5, and committed fraud, negligence, and breach of fiduciary duty in violation of state common law in the offer of an investment contract—a security. The buyer alleged various acts of fraud by the agent in inducing him to buy the unit and in the services she performed or failed to perform thereafter. A federal appeals court sustained the claims against the agent, holding that the rental pool arrangement was an investment contract and was therefore a security. As a result, the real estate agent was deemed to be a securities salesperson and implicitly was unlicensed. The security, which was not marketed as a security, legally resulted because each "investor buys one share—a condominium—in a common venture that pools the rents from all of the units." The financial success of each participant's individual investment depended on a rental pool manager generating a return on investment for the entire rental pool's success. These are factors that can determine whether an investment offering amounts to a securities offering.

In the above example, a real estate agent got sued for something she did not think she was involved in and for events which she had no control over. In fact, the developer was a large household name insurance company with plenty of legal counsel. Why had no one raised a red flag about the alternative legal perspective applicable to the rental pool? Doubtless the broker thought a security was a stock that you buy from a stock broker and never imagined it could be a contract related to a condominium purchase. How could she have avoided this issue? Here is how: any time the word "investment" is used in promotional materials where someone else will be doing the work and the investor will be earning a passive return, you should seek out competent securities law counsel to review the materials and analyze whether a security is being offered. Real estate lawyers, for example, often are not trained to recognize these issues.

When Does an Offer Typically Occur?

In the life of a corporate entity, an offer of securities typically occurs any time after the corporate entity has been formed and the round of founding shareholders or equity holders has been determined. Once the corporate entity has been formed and founders have been identified, each new investor brought in to provide financing on a passive basis is protected by the securities laws. Thereafter, from start-up stage all the way to the point of corporate dissolution, and even during a bankruptcy, it is possible legally to make an offer of investment.

However, the offer of a security can also occur *before* the corporation is formed. The statutory definition of security includes a "preorganization certificate or subscription." Thus, at any time prior to incorporation, an organizer of a forthcoming corporation could solicit passive investments in the future enterprise and subject himself or herself to the jurisdiction of state and federal securities laws.

What You Must, Can, and Must Not Say

What you must, can, and cannot say in an offer of investment depends entirely on the context in which the offer is communicated. One factor is constant—the offeree must either receive all facts that are material to the offer or have the ability to obtain from the offeror all facts the offeree deems to be material. Public registered offers and private offers made to non-accredited investors must include a balanced presentation of positive and negative facts, which includes a disclosure of the risks of accepting the offer and the risks faced by the business. Public registered offers are usually communicated via a SEC or state-approved registration and prospectus disclosure form. Private offers can be communicated orally or in writing, and there is no required disclosure form.

How the offer is communicated and to whom are significant factors in determining whether the offer will be subject to an exemption from registration or will be required to be registered. No offer should be made to anyone unless the offeror has first determined that the offer can be made in compliance with state and federal registration or exemption from registration requirements. Planning and executing a strategy of compliance with the federal and state securities laws is imperative for the offeror and those that assist in making and communicating the offer.

For example, if an offer of securities is registered, it can be advertised in any jurisdiction in which the registration is applicable. It can be a nationwide federal registration, a state-only registration, or an offer registered in multiple states. Advertised offers by small revenue companies are typically required to be registered in each state where an investor is solicited. Generally, advertising by a company *before* a registered offering has been approved by regulators is a bad idea unless the company can demonstrate that it routinely advertises and the advertising has no relationship to the pending securities offering.

Differing rules and limitations apply depending on whether the offer is registered or is communicated pursuant to an exemption from registration, and then it depends on which exemption. For example, a one-page flyer offering an above-market return and little else almost always is deemed to be fraudulent or materially misleading by regulators and plaintiff's attorneys because it is unlikely that all material facts about the entity making the offer are simultaneously disclosed.

An offer that is made pursuant to an exemption from federal registration usually is not permitted to be advertised anywhere if the target audience is within the territorial United States, under current law, with several significant exceptions. Small company offerings "registered" under the SEC's Regulation A, which is an exemption from federal registration for offerings under fifty million dollars but which requires the offeror to submit an offering circular to the SEC for its review and comment, permit a testing of the waters of investor interest through limited in-state advertising. Regulation D Rule 504, which is an exemption from federal registration for offerings under one million dollars, also permits the offering to be advertised to accredited investors so long as the state law where the offer is made permits advertising to accredited investors only. New Rule 506(c), which was created by the SEC in response to the mandate of the JOBS Act, permits advertising of private capital raises to accredited investors, and there is no dollar limit. Existing Rule 506(b) prohibits general solicitation and advertising, allows an unlimited amount of capital to be raised, but requires all unaccredited purchasers (of which there can be no more than 35) to be sophisticated and knowledgeable about investments. Crowdfunding (the ability to raise small amounts of capital from many investors without regard for their sophistication) will also be permitted, and will allow for the limited advertising of an offer of investment through any media, including social media, so long as the total dollar offering is less than one million dollars, notice is filed with the SEC, and provided that no investor funds more than the limit allowed for them according to a schedule of asset and income tiers in the statute.

The Truth, Material Facts, and Complete Backgrounds

Every investment offer must communicate only true facts. Not all facts about the offer and about the company making the offer must be disclosed, but all facts that would be material to an investor's investment decision whether to accept the offer and purchase the security must be disclosed. Thus, immaterial information is not required to be disclosed. There are also some strategic exceptions to the policy of full disclosure. For example, the rules applicable to federal registration statements (registered offers) allow certain information such as trade secrets and some vendor information, intellectual property, and matters of national security to be withheld.

What is material information always depends on the circumstances and it is impossible to categorize. The forms for registration statements and Regulation A offers drafted by the SEC and the small company offering registration form (SCOR) produced by the state securities commissions provide many categories of business and offer-related information, and these forms are a good reference for the preparation of written offers to be used in unregistered offers. The federal and state registration forms reference sets of regulations requiring the specifics of financial information, plans of operations, description of the securities offered, a ten-year employment description of all executive officers and board members along with disclosure of relevant financial litigation and corporate insolvencies that occurred on their watch, compensation of officers and directors, description of the company's business, physical plant or offices, competition, business strategic risks, investment risks, and other factors.

Generally, the large volume of information required to make an offer fully disclosed results in the drafting of a document that often is fifty to a hundred pages in length, and single line spaced. This document is called a "prospectus." Handbills, email notices or touts, billboards, flyers, and the like do not meet these standards of full disclosure because they typically identify only a few facts about the opportunity. The risk is that content-shallow methods of communication of offers can be viewed as being materially misleading in any one of a number of ways and can subject the offeror to significant penalties.

The material information required to be disclosed in a federal or state securities registration statement does not have to be the same information disclosed in a private investment offer. This is because in some private offers the only investors that are going to receive the offer are accredited; i.e., they have substantial income or assets and are presumed to be sophisticated. Disclosure obligations are relaxed to wealthy investors who because of their experience and wealth do not need the disclosure protection that the securities laws require. These people are believed to be capable of asking the right questions and of having sufficient economic leverage to obtain answers from company management. It certainly is permissible to prepare a full-blown, fully disclosed prospectus for presentation to accredited investors, and in certain circumstances (such as in advertised Rule 506(c) offerings), it would be prudent for the issuer to take that route. In other situations, such as in deals where only a couple of investors are participating and all are accredited, such persons are often provided with summary prospectii or so-called "big boy" letters, which are very brief descriptions of the offering and which usually also contain several paragraphs of cautionary warnings. If unaccredited offerees may receive the offer, the disclosure to all offerees should be enhanced to protect the issuer. In certain offerings, unaccredited investors must represent to the issuer that they are sophisticated and knowledgeable. If this representation is not made, then the unaccredited investor cannot participate in the offering.

SEC-filed registration statements and the SEC rules that govern the minimum material information required to be disclosed in a registration statement help set a guide post for the types and quality of information that must be disclosed to unaccredited investors in private offerings. This is because public registered offerings can be purchased by an unlimited number of unaccredited investors. Therefore, the information provided in a thoroughly disclosed private offering where unaccredited investors may be offerees or purchasers may very well be the same depth of disclosure as in a registered offering. Private offerings, though, have the flexibility to balance the depth and quality of disclosure (with certain limitations) against the cost of preparation of a full-blown federal registration statement. Disclosure in a private offering can be abbreviated in comparison to a federally-filed registration statement even when all of the offerees are unaccredited. Consider also that the less you wear the less you are protected from the elements. The same is true with disclosure documents. Going cheap and going shallow in disclosure may be more costly in the end if investors become unhappy and resort to the courts for relief.

In general, a public offer properly consists of a prospectus or offering circular or memorandum containing accurate and complete discussion of the following topics, the inclusion of financial statements (which may need to be audited), and the public availability of copies of various important contracts, agreements, opinions, and other material documents attached as exhibits to the registration statement or prospectus:

- The Company
  - Describes the state and date of incorporation and primary contact address and telephone number.
- Risk Factors
  - Factors from management's perspective that pose the greatest danger to causing the investor's potential loss of investment. Risks are usually characterized as risks of the business and risks of the investment.
- Business and Properties
  - Describes what the company does and intends to do, how and when it will do it or what its present status is, describes the company's

industry and competition and what type of competition is anticipated, dependence on certain customers, marketing strategy, backlog or status of production, number of employees and whether full or part-time, description of the property where business is conducted, whether it is owned or leased and all material terms, description of significant property items that may be assets such as patents or other intangible assets, tangible and real property, description of government regulatory environment in which the company is or will be, description of major corporate transactions such as mergers or acquisitions, and what milestones the company must achieve to be profitable if it is not already and consequences of delays in meeting targets.

- Offering Price Factors
    - Description of whether the offering price is a multiple of earnings, is based upon book value or another calculation, or is arbitrary, description of any conversion rights the securities may have, and a description of the issuer's recent securities sales and sale prices.
- Intended Use of Proceeds from the Offering and Dilution
    - Describes the percentage and amount of allocation of offerings proceeds raised to specified activities and shows how the allocations to activities will be made if the entire capital raise amount is not realized, whether any debts will be discharged using the proceeds, whether the issuer is also seeking other sources of capital, and describes what effects, if any, the offering will have on the existing shares or equities outstanding and authorized by the articles of incorporation.
- Capitalization
    - Describes the amount of short and long term debt owed by the issuer, shareholders' equity or deficit, amount of capital paid-in, number of shares of each class of equity authorized and issued and outstanding, and number of shares reserved for stock option or warrant exercises.
- Description of Securities
    - Describes the nature (debt, equity, or securities convertible into other securities) and terms of the securities being offered such as rights to

dividends, whether the securities are callable by the issuer, interest rate offered, etc.

- Plan of Securities Distribution
  - Describes the persons who will be making the offer to sell the securities and the extent to which those persons or entities are being compensated, describes any material relationships between the selling persons and management of the issuer, and whether there are resale restrictions on the securities.
- Dividends, Distributions and Redemptions
  - Describes whether in the prior five years the issuer has paid dividends or made other distributions of property rights to shareholders and whether it has bought back any of its securities.
- Officers and Key Personnel of the Company
  - Describes management by name, age, address, title, education, work experience and job function. Describes all negative issues in the prior ten years such as criminal convictions, finance-related regulatory proceeding orders and bars or limitations placed on activities, finance-related civil judgments, personal bankruptcies, and description of business that failed while this person was in a management role.
- Directors of the Company
  - Describes directors by name, age, address, title, education, work experience. Describes all negative issues in the prior ten years such as criminal convictions, finance-related regulatory proceeding orders and bars or limitations placed on activities, finance-related civil judgments, personal bankruptcies, and description of business(es) that failed while this person was in a management role. Describes whether directors are insiders (employees of the issuer) or outsiders, what percentage of time the director devotes to the issuer, and the extent to which the director is compensated (or indemnified) for service as a director.
- Principal Stockholders
  - iscloses by name all stockholders who own or have a beneficial interest in more than 5% of the issuer's voting stock, and describes how many

shares and what percentage of the issued and outstanding shares the person beneficially controls or has an interest in.

- Management Relationships, Transactions and Remuneration
    - Discloses marriage and blood relationships between officers, directors, key employees, and controlling shareholders. Discloses loans or other arrangements made to or from the issuer by these categories of persons. Discloses all forms of compensation received from the issuer by these persons in the last two years; describes all employment and indemnification agreements entered into between the issuer and these persons, and describes whether any of these persons has guaranteed any obligation of the issuer. Describes any arrangements designed to keep these persons from leaving the issuer, such as non-compete agreements, stock option vesting, or other incentives or restrictions. Also describes all plans providing for equity incentives available to employees, officers, or directors, how many shares remain reserved in such plans, and the duration of the plans.
- Litigation
    - Describes any pending or threatened proceedings believed to have or that may have a material impact on the issuer or that are brought against its officers, directors, or key persons.
- Federal Tax Aspects (for offerings by Subchapter S corporations)
    - Describe the nature and amount of anticipated Sub-S tax benefits and the material risks of their disallowance. Also, state the name, address and telephone number of any tax advisor that has passed upon these tax benefits.
- Miscellaneous Factors
    - Because the above list may not account for all material facts that are perceived by management as being relevant to investors, this section serves as a catch-all to disclose such matters.
- Financial Statements
    - These generally are comprised of a balance sheet, statement of cash flows, income, and stockholders' equity for the last two years and prepared using generally accepted accounting principles. If

pro forma balance sheets are appropriate because of a pending merger, acquisition, or divestiture of a material aspect of the issuer's operations, then a pro forma balance sheet should be provided showing the impact of the transaction on the issuer's financial statements.

- Management's Discussion and Analysis of Certain Relevant Factors ("MD&A")
  - This is a prose description that explains the financial statements, particularly if there are losses from operations, and management will describe steps being taken to correct the losses and identify the causes. The MD&A disclosure will describe any trends in operating results such as seasonal fluctuations, changes in the issuer's industry which may impact it, and describe the sales numbers for the period reported on. Comparative analysis is often provided with the same time period in the prior year with an explanation of the reasons why the results were better or worse. Management typically reports on the issuer's access to capital and capital needs in the MD&A disclosure.
- Exhibits
  - These include, for example, the corporate bylaws and articles of incorporation, a sample of the certificate being offered, any legal opinions issued for the offering, a blank subscription agreement for the offering, copies of significant contracts with the company which can include its property lease, agreements with underwriters or finders related to the offering, employment agreements with management, any plan of reorganization or acquisition or dissolution, any incentive plan or compensatory equity plan, copies of significant debt instruments, etc.

A private offer of investment *may* contain less information depending on the audience being solicited. The issuer contemplating making a private offering should prepare a full-blown "public" style offering memorandum when: (i) there are unaccredited investors who may receive the offer, and (ii) there is a general solicitation made to accredited investors with whom the issuer does not have a pre-existing relationship. The latter circumstance might include new Rule 506(c) (advertised) offerings made to accredited investors.

What Can You Say?

What you can say to prospective investors depends initially on which offering exemption you are using.

State Registered Offerings

In a state registered offering, you are generally permitted to advertise the offering locally. Only a limited amount of information may be given to offerees in the form of printed or radio and television ads or Internet communications. To advertise the offering in a state-registered offering conducted in compliance with Regulation A, you are permitted to say only:

- From whom the offering circular (prospectus) may be obtained;
- The name of the issuer of the security;
- The title of the security (e.g., common stock, debt, etc.);
- The amount being offered;
- The per unit offering price to the public;
- The identity of the general type of business of the issuer; and
- A brief statement as to the general character and location of its property.[7]

Applicable state laws may add to or reduce the permissible items in this list.[8]

This is slightly more than what the SEC allows to be communicated about federal registered offerings without the communication being deemed to be a prospectus.[9] Persons responding to the offering should be directed to acknowledge receipt of and to review the offering circular (or prospectus). After they have done

7 17 C.F.R. § 230.252.

8 It is possible that Rule 504 offerings conducted in compliance with new state-limited crowdfunding offerings may also be advertised in this manner.

9 The Securities Act of 1933, § 2(a)(10), excepts tombstone advertisements from registration requirements if they are limited to identifying from whom a written prospectus may be obtained, do no more than identify the security, state the price thereof, state by whom orders will be executed, and contain such other information as the SEC, by rules or regulation, may permit.

so, if they still have questions, only officers and directors and agents of the issuer can communicate with prospective investors. The communicator with prospective investors should be limited to one designated officer, director, or agent to avoid different or different degrees of information from being disseminated to different inquirers. The content of communications should be limited to what is in the prospectus to the extent possible unless disclosure is requested as to items deemed to be immaterial.

Private Unregistered Federal or State Offerings

The answer generally depends upon whether you are conducting a private offering under pre-JOBS Act rules such as Rule 506(b) or are using the new JOBS Act statutes and rules such as new Rule 506(c). The first communication depends upon whether you are using new Rule 506(c) or the pre-JOBS Act rules. The issuer or its legal counsel should select in advance of the offering which rules of exemption that it intends to qualify under. This choice will determine what activities are permissible to seek capital from potential investors.

New Rule 506(c)

Rule 506(c) allows for general solicitation and advertising to accredited investors and to raise an unlimited amount of capital. Thus, the issuer and its authorized officers, directors, and broker dealer agents can use social media, the internet, radio, print, or television to solicit accredited investors. What can they say in that solicitation?

Since the issuer only can seek accredited investors, that fact has to be communicated. In addition, it appears that no more information than what Regulation A offerings allow would be acceptable. This level of advertising is essentially a tombstone advertisement. See the section above for the list of Regulation A-permissible contents of a solicitation. Accredited investors should be solicited to answer questionnaires affirming their accredited status and directing them how to provide verification of their accredited status. If they qualify, they can then be shown the private offering memorandum. Thereafter, the designated officer, director, or broker dealer agent of the issuer can respond to any additional information requests the prospective investors may have.

Old Rule 506(b)

Rule 506(b) prohibits general solicitation and advertising, allows issuers to raise an unlimited amount of capital, but restricts to 35 the number of unaccredited investors who may be purchasers and requires that these purchasers must be sophisticated and knowledgeable about business matters. Offerings are limited to friends, family, and pre-existing relationships where the officers, directors, or broker dealer agents of the issuer have knowledge as to the financial status of the offeree.

How do you create a pre-existing relationship?

Let me start by saying what you cannot do, which many people do probably out of ignorance. You cannot advertise a meeting to people that you do not know where an issuer representative will be in attendance, even if the issuer will not be speaking about an investment opportunity, if you are handing out questionnaires at the meeting to later qualify prospects for a private offering. You cannot cold-call potential investors. You cannot buy a mailing list (even if it is a targeted list) and mail notices to the addressees.

Do you understand what this means? You cannot advertise the meeting with the company and then later try to qualify the attendees.

You can contact a small number of potential investors that you do not know if you have a reason to believe that they are qualified to invest or have invested in offerings similar to yours. You can also contact persons who may know qualified investors, if the referral sources would have reason to know that their contacts are qualified. As long as the issuer's officers, directors, and agents make connections in this manner and contact in the aggregate no more than perhaps 25 prospects, this may suffice as a "private offering." In this case it is the total number of persons contacted (offerees)—not the number of purchasers—that is important.

Between the contact and the investment, the issuer must confirm that the offerees are qualified as to their accredited or unaccredited status.

If you do not meet the private meeting or existing relationship criteria, you should not be speaking to anyone, if you are relying on Rule 506(b).

State and Federal Investment Crowdfunding

Using the federal investment crowdfunding exemption, issuers are able to use all means of communication to advertise their offerings, but they are limited to stating only:

- The name of the issuer;
- how much money the issuer is seeking, and
- who the authorized broker dealer or funding portal is.

State-limited crowdfunding is legal in 35 states and the District of Columbia, but there is not complete uniformity of the states' implementing statutes and rules. For example, in Kansas and Georgia, unaccredited investors are limited to investing $1,000 and $10,000, respectively, and the offering can be generally solicited. The maximum offering amount in both states is $1,000,000, and thus may qualify under SEC Rule 504's $5,000,000 exemption. Both statutes are deliberately structured to comply with the intrastate offering exemption under federal law (SEC Rule 147), which means that only companies incorporated in either state can be issuers, respectively, and only residents of either state can be investors, respectively.

These are the typical (but not universal) ways that issuers can legally solicit interest in private securities offerings.

Chapter 7

Who Can and Cannot Communicate with Prospective Investors

Certain Officers and Directors

Only officers and directors authorized by their corporation may communicate with prospective investors. Lower-level employees, equity holders that are not officers or directors, attorneys, or other agents of the corporation may not do so unless they are registered as securities broker dealers.

Indeed, no officer or director may be specially compensated directly or indirectly for communicating with prospective investors. They cannot receive commissions. They cannot receive success fees. No officer or director may have as his or her full-time job the position of communicating with prospective investors to obtain capital, unless that person is registered as a broker dealer.

Officers and Directors May Be Required to Register as "Brokers"

Generally, the federal and state definitions of "broker" are purposefully broad to include persons who are not compensated for introducing an investor to an investment opportunity. Anyone who engages in the activity of finding potential investors is a broker. Thus, corporate officers and directors who communicate with prospective investors are also brokers. Federal law, however, provides an issuer-employee exemption for participation in one offering per year. Also, most states exempt these persons from being required to register as brokers, provided that they are not compensated for their services as brokers and so long as it is not their full-time duty to raise funds for the corporation.

Certain states, such as New York and Nevada, may require corporate officers to register as brokers before they can seek investors in these states. New York requires corporate officers involved in soliciting New York residents to register as real estate brokers and to pay fees. If a company officer receives direct or indirect compensation for selling securities to Nevada residents, Nevada imposes an examination requirement on company officers, which the state may waive in its discretion.

Persons with Disqualifying Histories

Some people with histories of relevant criminal convictions, injunctions, cease and desist orders, or bars from the securities industry or from being an officer or director of a public corporation, or a penny stock bar are automatically barred under federal law and the laws of most states from participating in some but not all categories of unregistered securities offers. However, these same persons, unless they are barred from the industry, or have been barred from offerings of penny stock, may participate in *registered* securities offers. This is because registration statements require disclosure of material facts, and disclosure of criminal convictions, injunctions, and findings of violations in investment-related litigation are matters requiring disclosure, not preclusion.

Licensed Securities Brokers and Registered Portals

Licensed securities brokers can communicate on behalf of your company with investors, whether you are conducting a public, private, or crowdfunded offering, provided that your company has retained their supervising broker dealer to represent your company. Unlicensed "finders" or "consultants" or "agents" on the other hand should be avoided at all times. Unlicensed dealmakers are almost always uninsured, may have been barred by a regulatory body from participating in transactions in a particular industry, and certainly provide plaintiff's attorneys with a legal excuse to void their client's securities subscription in your company. Check the background of the agent at www.FINRA.org.

If your company is conducting an investment crowdfunding offering, the FINRA-licensed portal or platform that your company has engaged to conduct investor communications becomes the only entity that can communicate on behalf of your company to prospective investors. Make sure that the portal is registered at www.FINRA.org because an offering that was conducted on an unlicensed portal or platform is in danger of having to be rescinded and/or may be the subject of regulatory enforcement action.

Do it the right way. Keep the capital. Don't make a mistake here and have to give the capital back.

Chapter 8

WHO YOU SHOULD NOT SPEAK TO

If you are going to raise capital for your company in a private offering, you cannot communicate with anyone and everyone about the investment opportunity, as a general legal principle. The people you communicate with, whether face to face, by phone, video, email, messaging, snail mail, advertisement, etc., should be eligible to communicate with you and your company. Eligibility depends on the rules applicable to the specific exemption from registration that your company is using and the rules that may apply in the state where the investor resides. You may not be able to communicate with anyone in a particular state without first having complied with that state's notice-filing and/or broker registration requirements. Do your homework before going live with an offer.

Investor Residence

It is critically important to know the state in which a prospective investor resides before contacting him or her. This is because in some states the officers and directors who are soliciting investor interest may first have to be registered as brokers with that state, and, in most other states, in an exempt offering, payment of a fee and the filing of a notice may be required. (Sample state notice filings and a New York agent registration form are included in the Appendix.) In a federal registered offering for a smaller corporation, you need to know where you might conduct the offer because a state registration or qualification may also be necessary. Thus, if you are not going to register or seek exemption in a particular state, you should not communicate with any prospective investor in that state.

Age or Incapacity of Offeree

No one under eighteen years of age may independently purchase a security. This is because, as a general legal principal, minors do not have the legal capacity to enter into a contract, and the transaction in which a security is purchased in exchange for money is a contract. If a minor succeeds in purchasing a security, he or she can later seek rescission.

You should not try to sell your securities to an adult who is mentally infirm or who has been adjudicated as being mentally incompetent. Such contracts may be voidable by their guardians, personal representatives, or heirs.

Investor Status

In a registered offering of a security that trades on an exchange, any competent member of the public over the age of eighteen is eligible to purchase your security, as a general legal principle. In an exempt offering, you need to know whether the prospective investor is eligible, accredited or unaccredited, and in certain cases you also need to know whether he or she—or his or her investor representative—is knowledgeable and sophisticated in business matters. The knowledgeable-and-sophisticated qualification is required for unaccredited investors under SEC Regulation D Rule 506(b), but it is not required under SEC Rule 504. Some states have investor suitability requirements that must be followed when conducting a private offering. Look before you leap.

Unsolicited Inquiries from Prospective Investors

Law enforcement sting operations occur frequently, and typically target public company executives, among other securities industry targets. Company executives may be solicited to receive funding from a person posing as the representative of a private equity firm or hedge fund. Executives are baited to receive funding provided that they agree to "kick back" to the person a finder's fee or some other type of fee or commission, with the operative word being "kick back." The executives are being set up to violate the federal anti-kickback statute. People who fall victim to this government baiting program can look forward to up to five years in federal prison, suffering reputational damage on the internet, being sued by the SEC and barred for life from operating a public company. As a collateral consequence of a finance-related criminal conviction, convicted persons may find it difficult to open or maintain a bank account or brokerage account, or from obtaining a personal mortgage because financial institutions have perceived operational and regulatory risk when doing business with felons.

State securities commission staff sometimes pose as non-accredited investors. They may troll the internet, communicating through chat rooms or internet-based angel investor networks or funding platforms trying to engage corporate executives into offering to sell securities into their state where no registration statement or exemption notice has been filed or where company officers and directors have not registered as broker dealers. After a few telephone calls and probably email communications where company information has been delivered to the undercover agent, the trap is sprung and the company and its representatives may be charged as unlicensed securities brokers. Executives can easily be confused by this tactic as most states allow a sale of a *security* in their state if the offering is made under Regulation D, and a Regulation D offering notice has been filed with the SEC within fourteen days *after* the first sale in the state and payment of a fee. But brokers and dealers cannot make offers where they are not licensed and are required to be. Company executives typically do not see themselves as brokers because they are funding their own companies. Getting trapped and zapped by a state securities commission for a lack of securities registration or lack of broker registration has the collateral effect of: (1) forever putting one's name into the national securities enforcement database, (2) causing reputational damage that will be posted on the internet forever, and (3) perhaps statutorily disqualifying the company and the participating executives from conducting private raising of capital. If the state securities commission believes that the failure to register the offer was in some way deliberate, or that there was some misrepresentation made in connection with the offer, then criminal prosecution is a real possibility. A sample New York selling agent registration used by company officers is included in the Appendix.

Friends and Family

Contacting anyone—including friends and family—for interest in funding your venture is illegal unless a statute or administrative agency rule provides an exemption from registration of the investment offer (and the ability to solicit funds). How large is your family? How many friends do you have on Facebook? As stated above, many states have a limited offering exemption of approximately twenty-five purchasers. Federal law, under Regulation D Rule 506(b), permits up to thirty-five non-accredited purchasers in a single offering. Communications using interstate commerce with friends and family under these thresholds is permissible, but in both state and federal exemption schemes you must have a pre-existing relationship with the offerees. If you do not actually know the "friends" or "family" before contacting them, and you communicate with them with the ultimate goal of seeking their investment interest, that is an unregistered, non-exempt public offering. It only takes a single stranger in the mix to void the ability to claim the exemption.

There is more to this restriction. You are permitted to contact friends, family, and others with whom you have a relationship, provided that you are knowledgeable of whether they are accredited or unaccredited investors. This point is very important. If you contact too many unaccredited investors, and/or you (or the other officers or directors or broker agents of the issuer) do not actually know them, you can void the ability to conduct a private offering and subject yourself and everyone involved in the offering to liability.

Another alternative, albeit substantially more expensive, is to submit a Regulation A offering circular and notice to the SEC and to each state where you wish to seek funds from unaccredited prospective investors. Getting state approval may be difficult or impossible in some states because many conduct a merit review—a requirement that the offeror demonstrate a certain number of years of revenue before approval will be given. But if the offering receives appropriate approval, you will be able to advertise the offering in the states where approval was given. You can offer in more than one state but will need approval from each state of the offering circular. There is a limit of five million dollars combined in all states.

Under the Jumpstart Our Business Startups Act of 2012, two new exemptions from registration were created. One is new Regulation D Rule 506(c). New Rule 506(c) permits an advertised exempt offering anywhere in the United States provided that the only purchasers are verified as having met the definition of "accredited investor." There are no dollar limits on a Rule 506 offering.

The other exemption is the creation of investment "crowdfunding," patterned after a program in use in the United Kingdom and Australia. Under investment crowdfunding, a company that does not already have a class of securities registered with the SEC may use any means available to contact prospective investors, provided that no more than one million dollars is raised in a twelve-month period. There are caps on the dollar amount that an investor can invest, and the issuer must direct all prospects to its funding "portal" or its licensed broker dealer to obtain more information about the offering. Crowdfund issuers cannot accept investment funds directly from the public. All investments must be made through the issuer's broker dealer or its funding portal.

Both Rule 506(c) and crowdfunding have unique potential risks to the companies that utilize them, so, as always, caution is necessary before journeying into these realms without counsel.

Numerical Limits of Offerees

If there are too many recipients of your company's investment offer, that fact alone can make the offering ineligible for the registration exemption that you had planned around. Yes, you can tweet it and email blast it around the world to billions of strangers—if your offering was designed to be distributed in compliance with the rules applicable to a specific registration exemption. But what if you offered it to more than 35 unaccredited investors and accepted investment funds from less than 35 unaccredited investors? If your offering is compliant with Rule 504 you may still be in compliance if no applicable state securities laws have been violated. But your offering may not be eligible for the Rule 506(b) friends and family exemption and the federal preemption that this rule enjoys.

The different registration exemptions often have explicit limits on the number of purchasers but may have implicit limits on the number of offerees. There are also outer boundary statutes that limit the total number of shareholders a company can have before the company is automatically required to file quarterly and annual reports with the SEC. Make sure you know how many people are able to see or hear your investment offer and where they are located. Make sure you have not over-offered.

Chapter 9

METHODS OF COMMUNICATING FINANCIAL OFFERS

Generally speaking, for non-NASDAQ or larger companies, unless a federal and/or a state registration statement is in effect in the state in which investor interest is being sought, it is illegal to communicate an offer of investment to the public through *any* media. Thus, one answer to the question of what can you say to a prospective investor is *nothing*, if the offer is not registered. How then are offers made without the time and expense of registering a securities offering? Do friends and family offers need to be registered? Do you need a registration statement to seek capital from one potential investor for a real estate purchase? The answers to these common questions depend on how you go about it. There are several alternatives with each variety dependent on compliance with the particular exemption from registration you have chosen. These alternatives are summarized in Chapter 10.

There is one extreme way of avoiding federal registration requirements altogether for a solicitation for funds: communicate the offer orally in a face-to-face conversation in which the offeror and the offeree are situated in the same state. If you tell someone in a face-to-face conversation where no means of interstate commerce are involved, perhaps in a closed room, that communication is exempt from registration. However, if you invited them to the room using any means of interstate commerce, such as the mail, telephone, or internet, that type of communication invokes federal jurisdiction under the commerce clause of the U.S. Constitution. Thus, to utilize the oral offer exclusion from federal registration, you would in all probability have to be in the same state with a person with whom you are having the conversation. If one person was standing in Missouri at the state line and the other person was a few feet away standing in Kansas, an oral investment solicitation from one to the other would be an interstate communication for which registration may be required.

If the offeror and all offerees are in the same state, then even if the mails, phones, or internet are used in the solicitation process, there is a federal exemption for intrastate-only transactions. Do the states require registration of oral offers? The question is usually academic because most states have a "limited offering exemption," usually ranging between twenty-five to thirty-five purchasers, before a requirement of registration would apply. Check your state's law.

The flip-side of this chapter is that if the offering qualifies for a particular exemption from registration, you can use all methods of communication permissible in the exemption. Also, keep in mind that we are talking only about the registration requirements and exemptions from registration in this chapter. Federal and state anti-fraud statutes apply to every investment offer, whether oral or written, whether registered or unregistered.

Chapter 10

How Much Capital Do You Need? Exemption Planning

This is an important question. One rule of thumb is that you should seek more than you need to provide a cushion to keep the corporation operating for at least one year, although no law requires this. Seeking less capital than you need obviously undercapitalizes the corporation and may set the business up for quick failure. Seeking what you need at the moment may not be the same dollar amount that you realize you need two or three months from now. Usually, most companies need more capital in the short-term until they generate sufficient revenues to be self-sustaining. Meanwhile, the corporation is generating expenses and using founding capital which may not last very long. Corporations that seek less than one million dollars are signaling to the professional investment community that they do not want outside equity participation. Ultimately, obtaining excess capital might present a temptation for executives to pay themselves unwarranted bonuses or expending funds on items that ordinarily would be unthinkable, such as holding the company annual meeting at a resort destination or buying expensive "company" cars. These are the kinds of things that incite investors into launching lawsuits and complaining to regulators. Executives need to determine how much cash they need; who they can get it from, and then work within an offering registration exemption to keep capital-raising costs to a minimum.

The Pros and Cons of Private Offer Exemptions[10]

Regulation D Rule 504

Rule 504 is a transaction exemption that has two applications. It can result in a state-limited offer with the issuance of restricted securities, or if offered in a state which allows advertised sales of securities to accredited[11] investors, then the securities can be resold by the investor as free trading securities. The problem is that today no state has a statute that provides for the advertised sales to accredited investors. Therefore, any securities sold pursuant to the Rule 504 exemption can only be issued as restricted securities. This means that the purchaser cannot resell them publicly unless she registers her re-sale offer or is able to qualify her re-sale offer using an exemption from registration.

Rule 504, unlike the other rules under Regulation D, does not limit the number of non-accredited purchasers. Because Rule 504 is aimed at facilitating capital raises for small companies, it has a five million-dollar cap on the dollar amount that can be raised. There are also significant disclosure requirements that must be made to non-accredited investors, generally which would result in the preparation and delivery to the prospective investor of a private placement memorandum in connection with the offer. An audited balance sheet is required if possible.

Unlike Rule 506, Rule 504 is promulgated under the authority of Section 3(b) of the Securities Act, which exempts the *class* of smaller issuer securities offered from federal registration. This has the practical effect of enabling a state-qualified

10 This list is not exhaustive. It omits all state offering exemptions and several federal exemptions.

11 An accredited investor is defined to include natural persons with an individual net worth, or joint net worth with a spouse, that exceeds $1 million at the time of the purchase, excluding the value of the primary residence of such person; natural persons with incomes exceeding $200,000 in each of the two most recent years or joint incomes with spouses exceeding $300,000 for those years; or businesses in which all the equity owners are accredited investors. This is a status based entirely on either an asset test or an income test. Thus, there is not a *procedure* by which one can become accredited.

or state registered offering done in conformity with Rule 504 to not need federal registration for each offering of the same class of securities of the issuer.[12] Thus, offers conducted pursuant to Rule 504 and qualified in multiple states may be exempt from a concern that such offers amount to a public distribution needing federal registration.

States can and do impose requirements on the sales agents of the companies issuing the securities such as broker registration requirements for company officers and directors. New York does so. A sample New York selling agent registration is included in the Appendix.

Regulation D Rule 506(b)

Rule 506(b) is a transaction exemption that requires all non-accredited purchasers to have "such knowledge and experience in financial and business matters that [they are] capable of evaluating the merits and risks of the prospective investment." It also has a limit of 35 non-accredited investors, but Rule 506(b) does not have a dollar limit on the amount of proceeds that can be raised. This makes Rule 506 the most flexible and probably the most useful Regulation D exemption to issuers. The benefit of Rule 506(b) is the unlimited dollar limit and the fact that Rule 506(b) carries with it a statutory preemption preventing any state from placing any requirements on a Rule 506(b) offering. This enables the corporation to raise capital in multiple states without worrying about the application of differing state-by-state requirements on offerings. States can and do impose notice filing and fee payment requirements on Rule 506(b) offerings and can impose requirements on the sales agents of the companies issuing the securities such as broker registration requirements for company officers and directors. (Sample state notice filings and a New York selling agent registration are included in the Appendix.) States always have the right to investigate fraud in the offer of a Rule 506(b) offering, but states do not have the right to charge participants in a Rule 506 offering with selling unregistered securities.[13]

---

12 The SEC contends, however, that Section 3(b) of the Securities Act of 1933 is to be interpreted as an exemption for the offering only and not as a class registration exemption.

13 There is an unsettled legal question whether the issuer has the burden to prove the preemption of federal law and the bona fides of compliance with Regulation D Rule 506 as a threshold to rightfully claiming the exemption, or whether the issuer's claim to utilize Regulation D Rule

New Regulation D Rule 506(c)

New Regulation D Rule 506(c) is a transaction exemption that allows the corporation to advertise the offering for purchase by accredited investors only. As with Regulation D Rule 506(b), there is no cap on the amount of funds an issuer can raise. Corporations utilizing Rule 506(c) will have to be able to demonstrate that they have verified that each purchaser is accredited. The con of new Rule 506(c) is that if the corporation has advertised the offering and a solitary unaccredited investor purchased a security, then the exemption is blown and the corporation has engaged in an illegal unregistered offering. This is a dangerous result for all company and broker participants in the offering.

Section 4(a)(5) Accredited Investor Exemption

Section 4(a)(5) of the Securities Act of 1933 provides that sales made to accredited investors are exempt from registration if the aggregate offering price of an issue of securities offered in reliance on this paragraph does not exceed the $5,000,000 amount allowed under Securities Act Section 3(b)(1), if there is no advertising or public solicitation in connection with the transaction by the issuer or anyone acting on the issuer's behalf, and if the issuer files a Regulation D notice. (A sample Form D notice is included in the Appendix.) The statutory exemption can be relied upon, but courts have held, and the SEC does view, the requirements of Regulation D's exemption for sales to an unlimited amount of accredited investors to be determinative of compliance with Section 4(a)(5). The SEC requires securities issuers to file Form D declaring which exemptions they are relying on. Section 4(a)(5) is also a box that can be checked in Form D. Issuers usually check the 4(a)(5) box and the box for any one or more of the Regulation D rules. Although there are not any SEC regulations detailing compliance requirements for an offering conducted pursuant to Section 4(a)(5), the SEC and securities practitioners tend to follow the requirements of SEC Rule 506. Pure reliance on Section 4(a)(5) as a federal exemption without compliance with the exemption requirements of Regulation D Rule 506 would subject the issuer to compliance with applicable state securities registration

---

506 is automatically sufficient to claim federal preemption and moot any question of non-compliance with state securities registration and exemption requirements for sales of securities.

and exemption requirements. Compliance with Regulation D Rule 506, on the other hand, statutorily exempts the issuer from compliance with state securities registration requirements.

Regulation A

Regulation A, as modified by the JOBS Act of 2012, provides for a fifty million dollar cap and allows for a public offering, which means that investors can be accredited or unaccredited. There is no holding period requirement for purchases of Regulation A securities; thus, they are immediately re-salable. This is significant because re-sales of securities acquired under offers made pursuant to Sections 4(a)(2) or 4(a)(5), Regulations A, D, or S, and crowdfunded offers all must demonstrate that the issuer is at the time of re-sale in compliance with information disclosure requirements before the securities can be resold. Therefore, every investor purchasing securities in a Regulation A offering can be liquid immediately. However, if the offering conducted under Regulation A is limited to accredited investors, the offering preempts state offering registration requirements. On the other hand, offerings under Regulation A that include unaccredited investors must comply with each state's filing and review process.

Investment Crowdfunding

The investment crowdfunding exemption created by the JOBS Act of 2012 is unique in many respects. It allows issuers to raise a total of one million dollars through small investment amounts of capital from up to two thousand domestic investors with advertising and without concern for the investor's accredited or non-accredited status. One con is that unsophisticated issuers may let in hundreds of investors with whom they have no pre-existing relationship; of whom they have no knowledge of their investment goals, and cannot know their propensity for litigation. Another con is that there is no statutory incentive for the issuer to prepare and publish its financial information, which then prevents availability of SEC Rule 144 for the investors to resell their securities in public markets. Also, because the intent of crowdfunding is to enable the issuer to communicate directly with the public to keep costs of raising capital to a minimum, the usual gatekeepers—attorneys, accountants, and investment bankers—may be kept out of the loop. The problem with that scenario is that this disincentivizes the issuer from utilizing the very same group of professionals whose duty and practice it is to make sure that investors are protected through a fully disclosed offer. Thus, we are on the verge of unleashing thousands of tweeted, but probably not fully disclosed, crowdfunded offers for investment funding. This can cause a tsunami of fraud litigation and defeat the very purpose of providing a simple and inexpensive means for small companies to raise capital.

Federally authorized crowdfunding may have application for the small corporation that otherwise would avail itself of a Regulation A or D offering, wishes to avoid state and federal review, wants to advertise the offering, would limit investors to those having accredited status but not necessarily require them to be knowledgeable and sophisticated, will comply with the disclosure requirements of Regulations A or D, and will remain compliant with financial disclosure requirements such that investors will be able to exit through Rule 144. Under this scenario, a crowdfunded offer could be similar to the New Rule 506(c) exemption, but could avoid the risk that one non-accredited investor slipped through the cracks and voided the exemption. However, there will be a cap of one million dollars on the crowdfunded offer, while existing Rule 506(b) and new Rule 506(c) have no dollar cap on the offering amount.

A majority of states have enacted their own crowdfunding statutes. Generally, state crowdfunding statutes and rules permit offerings to be conducted by companies incorporated in the state provided that no more than $1,000,000 is raised and that investors are residents of the same state. Thus far, it appears that few companies have attempted to raise crowdfunded capital in an intra-state crowdfunding offering.

Section 4(a)(2)

Securities Act of 1933 Section 4(a)(2) permits transactions by an issuer not involving a public offering. Section 4(a)(2) is typically relied upon by public reporting companies whose securities are listed for trading at a national securities exchange (such as the New York Stock Exchange) and who issue restricted stock periodically to employees or vendors in lieu of cash payment for wages or invoices. It may be possible to rely upon Section 4(a)(2) at the federal level by the issuer who has failed to comply with some aspect of Regulation D, A, or S. Case law interpreting Section 4(a)(2) suggests that courts may look to Regulation D to determine whether the offer in question was a private offer. Controlling case authority holds that an offering to fewer than 100 investors is private so long as the investors have access to the same information that company management has. While issuers can rely on Section 4(a)(2) as an exemption at the federal level, offerings conducted pursuant to Section 4(a)(2) are not exempt from state securities registration and exemption requirements, unless the issuer's securities are listed on a national securities exchange.

Rule 701

This is the "sweat equity" rule. It allows private companies to compensate employees with company securities as payment for services provided that the company is not a reporting company with the SEC but has a written compensatory benefit plan (or written compensation contract) in effect when the securities are issued. The plan must have been established by the issuer, its parents, its majority-owned subsidiaries or majority-owned subsidiaries of the issuer's parent, for the participation of their employees, directors, general partners, trustees (where the issuer is a business trust), officers, or consultants and advisors, and their family members who acquire such securities from such persons through gifts or domestic relations orders. Compliance with Rule 701 still requires compliance with applicable state securities statutes governing offers and sales of securities. There is an annual limit of authorized Rule 701 securities issuances, which cannot exceed the greater of $1,000,000, 15% of the total assets of the issuer, or 15% of the outstanding amount of the class of securities being offered and sold in reliance on this rule, measured at the issuer's most recent balance sheet dated before the issuance.

Rule 1001, the California Exemption

Offers and sales of securities that satisfy the conditions of paragraph (n) of § 25102 of the California Corporations Code are exempt from federal registration, provided that the sum of all cash and other consideration to be received for the securities does not exceed $5,000,000, less the aggregate offering price for all other securities sold in the same offering of securities.

California Corporations Code § 25102(n) exempts from registration offerings by California business entities having only one class of voting class of stock outstanding at the end of the offering and whose sales are made to qualified purchasers defined as a natural person who, either individually or jointly with the person's spouse, (i) has a minimum net worth of two hundred fifty thousand dollars ($250,000) and had, during the immediately preceding tax year, gross income in excess of one hundred thousand dollars ($100,000) and reasonably expects gross income in excess of one hundred thousand dollars ($100,000) during the current tax year or (ii) has a minimum net worth of five hundred thousand dollars ($500,000). A general announcement of proposed offering may be published by written document only, provided that the general announcement of proposed offering sets forth only certain basic information specified in the statute (but is similar to a Regulation A tombstone advertisement).

Regulation S

Regulation S is available only for offers and sales of securities outside the United States. Securities acquired overseas, whether or not pursuant to Regulation S, may be resold in the United States only if they are registered under the Act or an exemption from registration is available. Regulation S securities need to remain offshore at least one year before being sold into the United States unless they are included in a registration statement and are registered for resale before the expiration of the one year holding period. Use of Regulation S can be feasible if the issuer has international business or has arranged for the placement of its securities through a domestic broker dealer having international investor clientele.

Chapter 11

WHAT IS THE ROADMAP TO RAISING CAPITAL WITH THE LEAST LITIGATION RISK?

Plan A: Reliance on Rule 506(b)

As you can see from Chapter 10, there are numerous potential exemptions that could be used in the planning of a capital raise. The most frequently used exemption that I am aware of is Regulation D Rule 506(b) .[14] This is the *old* Rule 506 exemption, which does not permit advertised private offerings. Use of this exemption has predominantly been for issuers soliciting investments from accredited investors only, as the SEC believes that only 11% of all Rule 506 offerings conducted between 2009 and 2012 contained non-accredited

14 For the year ended December 31, 2012, 16,067 issuers made 18,187 new Form D filings with the SEC, of which 15,208 relied on the Rule 506 exemption. Based on information reported by issuers on Form D, there were 3,627 small issuers relying on the Rule 506 exemption in 2012. This number likely underestimates the actual number of small issuers relying on the Rule 506 exemption, however, because over 50% of issuers declined to report their size. *See,* SEC Securities Act Rel. No. 33-9415 (Jul. 10, 2013).

purchasers.[15] Another interesting statistic is that more than two-thirds of Rule 506 offerings have ten or fewer investors, while less than 5% of these offerings have more than 30 investors.[16] Rule 506(b) permits up to 35 non-accredited purchasers in an offering. All non-accredited purchasers must be sophisticated and knowledgeable about business matters.

SEC data for the years 2009-2014 shows that Rule 506 offerings comprised 94.8% of all Regulation D offerings and accounted for 99.2% of the capital raised using the Regulation D exemption.[17] Issuers relying on Rule 506(c) accounted for only 2.1% of the Rule 506 capital raised from September 2013 through December 2014.[18]

The roadmap starts with ascertaining how much capital you believe you will need to: (i) sustain operations for the next twelve months if you are financing your business, (ii) acquire and run a business unit perhaps for several years before you can flip it, or finance and maintain a real estate acquisition until you can flip it.

Although the vast majority of private capital raises conducted using the Rule 506(b) exemption utilized funding obtained from accredited investors only, these investors need to be qualified such that the issuer reasonably believes that they are *in fact* accredited. The first step in limiting litigation risk is to decide that the capital raise will be limited to accredited investors only. The checklist/questionnaire will be useful for your understanding of what is needed and will help you prepare and plan the offering. (Of course, I recommend that you plan and prepare for your specific needs with competent securities legal counsel.)

Rule 506(b) Capital Raise Checklist/Questionnaire

The following section is both a checklist and questionnaire designed to take you through the process of planning a private offering to accredited investors only using Regulation D Rule 506(b). This list and questionnaire will perhaps help you to think about, and raise questions about, your preparedness to conduct a

---

15 *Ibid.*

16 *Id.*

17 Bauguess, Gullapalli, and Ivanov, "Capital Raising in the U.S.: An Analysis of the Market for Unregistered Securities Offerings, 2009-2014," SEC whitepaper (Oct. 2015), available at www.SEC.gov/files/unregistered-offering10-15.pdf.

18 *Ibid.*

capital raise. This list and questionnaire is a guide only. It is not a one size fits all prescription. You and your company will need to tailor and possibly expand this list to suit your specific needs.

1. Determine how much cash you need and in what time frame.
2. Retain the assistance of competent legal counsel.
3. Has more than six months passed since the last offering by your company or a parent company, subsidiary, or an affiliated company?
    a. If yes, is a registered offering by your company or an affiliated company presently ongoing (or terminated in less than thirty days ago)?
        i. If no, you are eligible to use Rule 506.
    b. If no, then your offering may be integrated with an earlier offering with the potential consequence that the number of unaccredited purchasers or the limitation on total offering amount may exceed the allowed maximums and require a rescission offer to all purchasers.
4. Will the company be conducting another type of offering or financing while the private offering is being conducted?
    a. If yes, determine whether the financing must be integrated with the proposed securities offering. Consult counsel.
5. Has the company prepared its financial statements according to generally accepted accounting principles?
    a. Is the most recent completed period of accounting information less than one year old (and preferably less than six months old)?
    b. Do the financial statements include detailed notes to explain the background of the company, its capital structure, and special treatment accorded certain significant transactions?
    c. Are related party transactions identified?
    d. Have the financial statements been audited?
6. Has the board or majority shareholder executed a resolution authorizing the capital raise?
7. Ask all officers, directors, key employees, and all shareholders that own or control more than 10% of the company's voting equity shares to execute a fully-completed officer and director questionnaire. A sample

officer and director questionnaire is provided as a bonus offer for purchasing this book.

8. Determine whether anyone is disqualified from participation in an offering such that the Rule 506 exemption is unavailable to the issuer and another exemption must be relied upon, or whether the disqualifying event merely needs to be disclosed and the exemption is still available.
9. Determine who is authorized to speak to potential investors.
10. Draft an internal policy that each employee must sign to have them acknowledge which persons are authorized to speak to persons outside the company about investment matters, and how to handle outside inquiries. Determine the length of time that the offering will be open, whether and in what circumstances the offering period will be extended, and what approvals will be needed from purchasers to extend the offering to others or to allow additional time for initial offerees to fully subscribe.
11. Have you prepared projections?
    a. For use of proceeds, prepare a projection that identifies where the funds raised will be allocated when 100%, 50%, and 10% of the fundraising goal is achieved. This information should be assumed to be made available to potential investors.
    b. For sales or revenues, if you prepare a projection, determine whether or not to make it available to prospective investors.
        i. If you will make it available, make sure that legal counsel has reviewed it for disclosure of assumptions and the reasonableness of assumptions.
        ii. If you intend not to make it available, create a procedure to limit access so that not a single prospective investor accidentally views it.
12. Determine if you are willing to accept unaccredited investors into your company, whether as debt or equity investors. This checklist assumes that you choose not to do so. (Additional procedures would be required if you choose to accept unaccredited investors. These additional procedures would require enhanced information disclosures by the issuer and seek

additional information about the knowledge level and sophistication of the unaccredited investors.)

13. In which states will you solicit investors?
    a. Determine if any affected state requires pre-filing of offering documents and officer and director registration before offers can be made in that state.
    b. Determine filing fees for subparagraph (a) above.
14. Do you already know who your probable investors are?
    a. If not, determine how will you locate and legally solicit an investment from prospective investors.
    b. What evidence do you have that each intended offeree is accredited?
        i. Develop an offeree list based upon knowledge by issuer or issuer's agents of each offeree's qualifications.
        ii. Determine that issuer or its agent has a sufficient relationship with the offeree to confirm offeree's qualifications.
    c. Determine how many persons are you intending to solicit.
        i. If you target too many (including accredited investors), the offering could be deemed to be illegal because statutory requirements mandate registration of the offer, and therefore the Rule 506(c) exemption cannot be used.
    d. Create a procedure that the authorized officers, directors, and agents must follow:
        i. about who—or the types of persons—that they can communicate with about the offering and what they can say about the company and the offering,
        ii. advising them against communications with unaccredited investors and those not cleared by the screening process,
        iii. what the authorized persons are authorized to say to prospective investors, and
        iv. how to document contacts with prospective investors.
    e. Prepare and distribute an investor questionnaire to screened investors to confirm accredited status of prospective offeree.
    f. Screen the responses to make sure that all responders are qualified.

   i. Reject unqualified responders from further communication pertaining to the proposed accredited-investors-only offering.

15. Have the founding or early equity holders executed a shareholder's agreement or operating agreement? (Operating agreements and shareholder's agreements are often used to memorialize private understandings about issues concerning buyout and transfer of equity interests, restrictions of resale or transfer, dispute resolution, director deadlock, election or appointment of directors, minority equity holder rights, tax treatment, permissible business practices or limitations on the industries in which the company can participate, etc. Prospective members of a limited liability company are typically expected or required to join the operating agreement. Prospective equity investors in a c-corporation may or may not be expected or required to join a shareholder's agreement.)
    a. If no, consult legal counsel about your company's and founder's circumstances. The best time to resolve end-of-company distributions, passage of title to a spouse, buy-out rights, etc. is at the beginning of the company when all participants are friendly and agreeable.
    b. If yes, will prospective investors be required to join the shareholder's agreement or operating agreement?
    c. Whether or not new investors are required to join an existing agreement, the shareholder's agreement or operating agreement should be made available to prospective investors.
16. Have you structured the articles of incorporation and bylaws to achieve objectives such as the ability to redeem shares, structure certain classes of equity with voting or non-voting rights, prevent takeovers, and indemnify officers, directors, employees, and agents, etc.?
    a. If no, consult legal counsel about your company's and founder's circumstances. Companies aspiring to be publicly traded in the future may find it easier to prepare their articles of incorporation and bylaws sooner rather than later when there may be many more shareholders with a say on corporate structure. Companies not aspiring to be public may want protections in the articles and bylaws to guarantee certain

benefits in case of disputes between officers, directors, and controlling shareholders. Discuss and resolve these issues early in the company's existence.

17. Implement an initial framework of internal control procedures with your accountant's assistance.
    a. Ensure that a numbered securities certificate issuance register is created that also records all numbered securities received for cancellation.
    b. Create a procedure requiring that all certificates issued as evidence of the investment contain a restriction-on-transfer notice. This will help ensure that holders of certificates and potential buyers are made aware that the shares may not be freely tradable and additional information is needed before a sale of these shares is consummated.
    c. Create a procedure whereby the employee in charge of the company's securities–register or investor-list does not issue any certificates without written authorization from a c-level authorized executive or a written opinion from the issuer's securities counsel.
18. Choose which registration exemption(s) you wish you qualify for. (This list assumes you have chosen Regulation D Rule 506(b)).
    a. Commence the process of organizing corporate records, material contracts, agreements, and documents. (A Sample Due Diligence Checklist is included as a bonus for purchasing this book.)
19. Are there related agreements outstanding that may be affected by the capital raise, such as warrant agreements, stock option agreements, registration rights agreements, rights of first refusal, and non-dilution agreements?
    a. All such agreements should be reviewed for potential compliance issues.
    b. All such agreements should be made available to prospective investors.
20. Determine whether the offering disclosure and subscription will be by "big boy" letter or by private offering memorandum with attached subscription agreement.
    a. Commence preparation of the offering document and subscription agreement.

b. Create a procedure to ensure delivery of the document to the intended addressee.
c. Number each document and create a list to associate the numbers to specific offerees.
d. Records should be established:
    i. Date of delivery of offering documents to potential investors;
    ii. The dates when, and the types of additional *material* pieces of information that were provided, including any oral disclosure, to requesters;
    iii. The dates when the additional items in subparagraph (ii) above were provided to offerees who have not yet subscribed; and
    iv. The dates when the additional items in subparagraph (ii) above were provided to purchasers in the offering along with a statement that if the additional disclosure would cause the purchaser to change his or her mind, then the purchaser has ____ days (your choice) to rescind the purchase.
e. Ensure that appropriate state and federal cautionary statements are included in offering materials.
f. Ensure that applicable state rescission notices are contained in the offering materials and in the subscription agreement.
g. Ensure that restrictions against resale are disclosed in offering materials and acknowledged in the subscription agreement.
h. Ensure that the purchaser's investment intent and accredited status are represented in the subscription agreement.
i. Create a procedure requiring that before the issuer accepts a subscription, a documented telephone call to each investor who returns a subscription agreement with payment will occur as to the investor's past investment and trading practices and current plans to invest or resell the security subscribed for.
    i. Reject any investor who does not have investment intent.

21. Determine whether there will be a minimum funding amount that must be raised before any proceeds can break escrow.

a. If there will be a minimum offering amount, obtain a third-party escrow agent.
    i. Execute a written escrow agreement with the escrow agent that prevents the release of escrowed proceeds until the minimum proceed threshold has been met or to return proceeds after a stipulated time period if the minimum is not met.
    ii. The escrow agreement should be made available to prospective investors.

b. If there will not be a minimum escrow and all proceeds raised will be made available to the issuer, open a separate bank account for the offering, preferably at a bank that does not have an existing relationship with the company (in case an investor sues and tries to freeze company assets.) Thus, if there is a problem, the company's operating account(s) is less likely to be immediately affected.

22. Are you planning on issuing press releases or other announcements or advertising before or while the offering is going?
    a. If yes, run them all by competent legal counsel at a reasonable time before issuance for a legal compliance review.
    b. If not, save money on lawyer's fees.
23. Select a SEC EDGAR-system filing agent to file Form D with SEC.
    a. Apply for filing codes with SEC
    b. Prepare and file Form D no later than within 15 days of first sale, unless Form D was filed in compliance with a state requirement to pre-file Form D and obtain clearance of selling agent and offering notice in a state that requires such filings and registrations prior to an offering being conducted in such state. (A sample Form D, state notice filing forms, and a New York selling agent registration form are included in the Appendix.)
    c. Create a procedure and calendar reminder for the Form D to be reviewed periodically and at least annually for any needed amendment.
24. If required, commence state registration of selling officers.
25. Commence distribution of numbered offering documents (prospectus and subscription agreement).

   a. Follow-up with each offeree no earlier than 4-6 weeks after distribution of offering materials.
26. Commence state notice filing and designation of agent for service of process in any state in which a sale occurs, if notice filing has not already been done.
27. Terminate offering upon achievement of capital raise limit or any date of offering termination, whichever comes first.
28. File final amendment to Form D within 30 days of close of offering.

Raising capital while limiting litigation risk starts with planning along the lines of this guide. There is more to it, of course. For example, if you review the bonus items available to purchasers of this book, the Sample Due Diligence Checklist, that document alone will open your eyes—depending on the stage of your business—to the documents that you may need, should have, or have no need of, that may be relevant to investors who may invest in your company.

Plan B: Reliance on Rule 504 and State Offering Exemptions

The Achilles' heel of Rule 506(b) is the requirement that all unaccredited investors must be knowledgeable and sophisticated. If one unaccredited purchaser is not sophisticated and knowledgeable—and this was reasonably known to the issuer at the time of purchase—the Rule 506(b) exemption would be blown and the issuer and individuals involved technically could all be subject to an investor claim of rescission and/or regulatory claims for injunctive relief, penalties and disgorgement. What is the fall-back position for the issuer?

Rule 504 seems to be an appropriate Plan B for the issuer. Rule 504 has no limit on the number of unaccredited purchasers as does Rule 506(b), and Rule 504 does not have any requirements for the knowledge or sophistication characteristics of unaccredited investors. However, Rule 504 has a $5,000,000 cap. The major drawback of Rule 504 is that it requires simultaneous compliance with state registration or exemption requirements in each state where there is a purchaser, and the $5,000,000 cap places an arbitrary limit on the dollars that can be sought and raised; whereas, Rule 506 offerings are exempt by statute from state securities offering restrictions.

Most states have an exemption from registration that is meant to be used simultaneously with the Rule 504 exemption. Compliance with such exemptions is made difficult simply due to the fact that the laws of each state where a purchase occurs and their respective fee payment and review procedures must be consulted to determine the means for legal compliance. This is not necessarily insurmountable, provided that the offering can comply with an available offering exemption in each state in which the offering is made, and assuming that officer and director registration requirements have been complied with, if applicable.

Rule 504 trumps Securities Act of 1933 Section 4(a)(2) as a fallback plan in many respects (as discussed earlier). Among other reasons, because Rule 504 is a rule, compliance with the requirements of the rule are simpler because they are distinctly stated. An issuer can read the rule and related Regulation D requirements identified in Rules 501 and 502 and know what is required. Likewise, compliance with state exemption requirements is oftentimes straightforward in the sense that states often have a small offering exemption that corresponds with the requirements of Rule 504. A state exemption from registration may or may not be specifically available for a Section 4(a)(2) exemption discussed below because a state may not have an exemption that precisely fits the court-driven requirements evolving under Section 4(a)(2).

Plan C: Reliance on Securities Act Section 4(a)(2)

Reliance on Section 4(a)(2)) as a stand-alone private offering exemption in my view is more perilous than reliance on the Rule 506(b) or Rule 504 exemptions discussed as Plans A and B above. The reasons are these: Section 4(a)(2) lacks the specificity of what you cannot do and the descriptions of terms found in Regulation D Rules 502, 504, and 506(b), and state offering exemptions must be found in each state where securities are offered. By being vaguer than Regulation D, Section 4(a)(2) leaves compliance with its terms subject to court precedent, which develops over time and is inherently less precise than following the complexity of Regulation D's requirements. Another drawback is that while issuers may be able to rely on Section 4(a)(2) as an exemption at the federal level, offerings conducted pursuant to Section 4(a)(2) are not exempt from state securities registration and exemption requirements, unless the issuer's securities are listed on a national securities exchange. Since most corporation finance offerings are not registered on national securities exchanges, Section 4(a)(2) offerings must also comply with a limited offering exemption or other exemption in the state where the offeree resides.

Court opinions, rather than precise securities commission regulations, are the guideposts to compliance with the Section 4(a)(2) exemption. From a planning standpoint, reliance on case law, in contrast to reliance on the requirements of a precise regulation, is more difficult because the next case that is decided could disfavor the manner in which an issuer has conducted an offering. Nevertheless, the reported court opinions that discuss Section 4(a)(2)) have made clear that what distinguishes a private offering from a public offering is whether the offerees have access to the kind of information that a full blown offering registration statement would contain. Unlike Rule 506(b)'s requirement that all unaccredited investors must be sophisticated and knowledgeable, federal courts have held that under Section 4(a)(2), the offeree's sophistication may be irrelevant if the offeree did not have the ability to access the level of information known to senior executives of the issuer. Moreover, at least one appellate court has stated that officers of the issuer, if they were not in a position to access all pertinent information relevant to an offer of the issuer's securities, were in need of full disclosure. On the other hand, a court has held that evidence of the offeree's economic bargaining power—the offeree's ability to negotiate the terms of the offer—is sufficient proof that the offeree had the ability to access inside information if desired. In lieu of actual disclosure of information to an offeree, to rely on the Section 4(a)(2) exemption, the issuer must be prepared to prove that all offerees occupied a privileged position relative to the issuer that afforded them the opportunity for effective access to information that a registration statement would otherwise provide.[19]

The case of *Doran v. Petroleum Management Corp.*, 545 F.2d 893 (5th Cir. 1977), provided a wealth of guidance on the requirements of Section 4(a)(2). The court first articulated that several important factors determine whether an offering is private and exempt from registration: (1) the number of offerees and their relationship to each other and the issuer; (2) the number of units offered; (3) the size of the offering; and (4) the manner of the offering.

---

19 See, e.g., *Doran v. Petroleum Management Corp.*, 545 F.2d 893 (5th Cir. 1977).

The Number of Offerees

The Court explained that the number of offerees is important to ascertain the magnitude of the offering and to determine the characteristics and knowledge of the offerees. An issuer claiming an exemption will automatically fail to prove *the exemption* if it cannot demonstrate with certainty the number of offerees. However, the number of offerees is not dispositive of whether the offering is private or public in nature, but the fewer the number of offerees, the more likely that this factor will favor the issuer.

Relationship to the Issuer

All offerees must have available to them the information a registration statement would provide. The sophistication of the plaintiff is irrelevant without proof that all offerees had available to them the requisite material information. Availability of information can mean either that the offerees received a disclosure of all material facts, or it can mean that the offerees had access to the files and records of the issuer or the ability to have their questions answered, which can be because of their employment position with the company or bargaining power. The ability to access information is conditioned upon proof that the investor was sufficiently knowledgeable and sophisticated about investment matters to know which important questions to ask. This factor can cut against the issuer if unaccredited offerees were solicited to invest.

Selective Disclosure

The court made clear that even proof of delivery of an offering document (a private placement or private offering memorandum) containing all material facts, *i.e.*, the facts disclosed in a registration statement, would not suffice to establish the Section 4(a)(2) exemption, in the absence of proof that all offerees received disclosure of all material facts.

Size of Offering, Number of Units, and Manner of Offering

These factors are more numerical in nature. Common sense dictates that a small dollar amount sought to be raised, a small number of units offered, and a communication about the offering made to only a few persons would all weigh in favor of a conclusion that the offering was of a small magnitude and therefore should be exempt from registration.

Doubtful Cases Do Not Qualify

Last, the court made clear that in cases where the evidence of disclosure of material facts to all offerees was doubtful, the court will deny the claim of exemption.

Thus, reliance on court opinions when structuring an offer can be trickier than following the guidance of Regulation D, and therefore in my view reliance on Section 4(a)(2) ranks it no higher than Plan C. Section 4(a)(2) is not *Plan D*, however, because I believe it does have its place as a tool available to an issuer in the right circumstances. There are two primary circumstances that come to mind: (1) as a possible backup plan in case an offering conducted using Plan A's Rule 506(b) or Plan B's Rule 504 requirements were not complied with (but state offering exemption requirements might not have been complied with in the latter case) according to the requirements of Regulation D, and (2) where the offerees are closely connected to the issuer's executive management.

The Section 4(a)(2) exemption *might* suffice as a backup plan. Because of Section 4(a)(2)'s vagueness, if an issuer failed to comply with the precise terms of Regulation D Rule 506(b) (or another exemption), and if the correct factual circumstances are present, an argument may be made that the offering legitimately remained exempt from the federal registration requirements because the offering complied with Section 4(a)(2). A private offering only has to meet the requirements of one exemption from registration to be exempt. (Many offerings qualify for multiple exemptions.)

Unfortunately, in most states, if the limit on 35 unaccredited purchasers has been exceeded, even if the Section 4(a)(2) exemption was available at the federal level, investor claims for rescission may be viable under state law, as would potential claims by state securities regulators.

The other use of Section 4(a)(2) is when payments in the form of company securities in lieu of cash are made to employees, consultants, or other vendors. In the small company scenario, all employees may have access to all material information. Likewise, company consultants such as attorneys, accountants, and engineers may have sufficient bargaining power, and knowledge of and access to material company information such that they effectively have the same information known to management. Company vendors may also know as much about the company as does management. For example, a website designer of an internet-based business may know exactly how well the company is performing from a revenue and marketing standpoint and how it compares to similar competitors. On a case-by case basis, any of these categories of persons having a relationship with the securities issuer may qualify as offerees for which a private offer can be made in compliance with Section 4(a)(2). The issuer would be wise to consult competent securities counsel to aid in this determination of eligibility.

Chapter 12

A Simple Real Estate Financing Example

As an example of a possible real estate scenario that can trigger the application of the securities laws, please consider the following fact pattern. A real estate investor locates a property but does not have the funds to acquire it. The investor contacts a number of banks, but finds only one or two banks willing to listen. The banks will not lend for more than a 65% loan-to-value ratio. The investor needs to cover the additional 35% with his or her own funds or funds from others. The investor has to personally guarantee the funds offered by the bank. What should the investor do?

A typical response is that the investor forms a limited liability company (LLC) and places an offer on the property in the name of the LLC. The investor telephones and emails family members and business associates seeking contributions to the LLC, and in doing so has changed his position to one of an investment promoter. The investor/promoter may need only one other investor and possibly as many as a half-dozen, depending on how much each one offers to contribute. How many laws has the investor/promoter just broken?

The answer depends on the amount of funds being sought, how many friends and family invested; how many states the offer was directed into, and how the offer was communicated. The dollar amount sought to be raised dictates the available options for exemptions and the applicable rules of each exemption from state and federal securities registration. The number of offerees, the number of purchasers, their relative sophistication, and their finances are other primary considerations.

The solicitation for funds was made to friends, family, and business associates. Were these people qualified as accredited investors? What did the investor/promoter know about their finances? Were they knowledgeable and sophisticated about business matters?

Did the investor/promoter become a broker? Not in most states, but Nevada and New York may require broker registration of the seller before an offer is communicated. Offering into different states without verifying whether broker registration in each state is required can void the entire offering under the local state law.

But on behalf of how many corporations has the investor/promoter made investment offers in the prior twelve months? Under federal law and the law of some states, there is a limit of one transaction per year before an "isolated" transaction will be viewed as being that of an unlicensed securities broker.

Did the investor/promoter and the LLC comply with applicable state and federal requirements applicable to Rule 506 offerings, for example? In a Rule 506 offering, the failure to file a Form D with the SEC within 14 days and comply with each state's notice filing fee and appointment of agent for service of process requirements can void the offering in that state. This is true because the states look for the filing of Form D as proof that the securities issuer is properly claiming the exemption that preempts state securities offering registration requirements. Private investors seeking to void a transaction can point to the issuer's lack of filing of a Form D, the issuer's failure to pay a notice filing fee, and/or the issuer's failure to file an appointment of agent for service of process form, if true, as possible grounds for rescission of the investment. Such items of non-compliance could result in a court concluding that rescission is warranted because these compliance items were material requirements of the issuer's claim of exemption.

The investor/promoter's offer was an offer of passive investment, most likely. No one would have to undertake an active role in the LLC. Their investment returns, if any, would be derived through the investor's efforts in choosing a property, supervising improvements to the property, and later selling it. Each contributor probably became a passive equity member of the LLC, which constitutes a security. That arrangement established securities law jurisdiction over the transaction. But we don't know what type of security was offered, nor do we know its terms.

The friends, family, and associates could have also been offered promissory notes instead of equity participation. In this case, what was the duration of the notes? Was a guarantee of repayment given? Notes that are of a term shorter than nine months are excluded from the definition of security. Such promissory notes are called "commercial paper" and are commonly associated with inter-bank loans. However, it is doubtful that unless the LLC was also a financial institution, it could be an issuer of commercial-grade paper. Promissory notes are also securities, so the investor/promoter has not avoided the securities regulation scheme. What if the investor/promoter caused the LLC to offer balloon mortgages to each successive offeree until the full amount needing to be raised was completed? If the mortgages were made in the names of individual investors, and the bank with the proposed first-position mortgage did not object, this could be a solution that avoids the application of the securities laws of some states. There would need to be a statutory exemption in the state exempting mortgages from being classified as securities, and the offering of multiple mortgages to finance the same project could still be seen as a common plan of financing that is subject to the federal securities laws. The more people who receive the offer, the more likely it is that the financing plan would be viewed as being a securities offering. Thus, the situation could become more complicated and might take significant legal expense to structure or determine that it cannot be done without compliance with the securities laws.

What if the investor/promoter puts together a list of potential investors from a real estate club membership list? Would this be a private offer if only the people on the list were contacted for their interest? Not under federal law. It is likely that at least one of the people on the list will be a stranger with whom the investor has no pre-existing relationship. And the use of lists is disfavored by the SEC which views lists presumptively to be an indicia of a general solicitation. Also, the investor/promoter does not know whether any of the listees are accredited or unaccredited. Before accepting their money, the investor/promoter would need to obtain sufficient personal financial information on each of them, and might also want information on their knowledge and business sophistication. Contacting that one stranger would constitute a public offering of securities, and would void the availability to claim exemption under Rule 506(b) (but not Rule 506(c)). Under the laws of some states, a limited offering exemption may exist if all of the offerees reside in the same state. If less than the minimum number of investors purchased the investment opportunity, then the offer could be compliant using Rule 504 and possibly under Rule 506(b) and 506(c), depending on whether there are non-accredited purchasers, compliance with the knowledge and sophistication requirement, and/or proof that all purchasers are accredited investors.

The federal intrastate securities offering exemption, which does not require any knowledge of the sophistication of the offeree, is not available if the investor/promoter solicited out of state prospects.

Other state exemptions could be used in parallel with an offer structured to comply with SEC Regulation D, Rule 504. However, if any of the offerees are unaccredited, the LLC will have to provide an audited balance sheet and possibly a prospectus to the offerees. This will take time to prepare and may not be workable due to time or budget limitations.

Including non-accredited investors in the deal creates too many issues and takes too much time. The better strategy is to have enough pre-existing, knowledgeable and sophisticated accredited friends and family available to support the transaction under Rule 506 (no dollar limit, no state requirements other than a notice filing and payment of a fee in most states). Consider using Rule 504- if you don't know any sophisticated and knowledgeable prospective unaccredited investors, but you do know unaccredited investors. Solicit from this category of investor as a last resort, and do so knowing that these types of people are the most likely to sue you and the company later on.

What about registering or qualifying the offer? The registration of the offer at either the state level or federal level will take too long. Generally, it takes at least thirty days before the SEC will provide comments on a registered offer. The states can take 90 days or longer before providing feedback. Registration, although safer in some respects, is too cumbersome for the speed needed in a real estate transaction.

What about the antifraud provisions? In the example, we do not know what was said to entice the prospective investors. Were they improperly guaranteed anything? What was disclosed about the property being purchased or the history of the investor/promoter? We do not know. Was a prospectus or private placement memorandum used that would disclose many facts about the investor, the LLC, the property, the illiquid nature of the investment, etc.? Probably not. A typical problem here is that, where there is no written disclosure document delivered to the prospective investor, there is only his or her word of what was said to induce the transaction versus the recollection of the original investor. Burned investors rarely remember being told about the risks of the investment and will swear they were not informed of risks and important background information. The investor/promoter will swear otherwise. What will a jury do? That is anyone's guess, but juries generally try to compensate those who they believe have lost money or been injured.

What are the risks to the original investor/promoter? In general, as a practical matter, if the transaction goes forward and the property returns principal and profit to the investors, it is unlikely that anyone will complain. It is typically when the transaction results in a loss to the investors that they will seek redress from those that induced them to invest. Rational promoters of real estate opportunities probably do not anticipate at the outset that their transactions will blow up and that law suits will be levied. Thus, the prudent investor/promoter will seek competent investment or securities counsel to ensure state and federal securities law compliance. Criminal prosecution for offers or sales of unregistered non-exempt securities is possible at the state level. Criminal prosecution is less likely at the federal level unless the funds at issue are large, probably in excess of one million dollars, or there is media interest in the debacle. Private suits can be a nuisance to the investor/promoter. If state securities laws are not pre-empted as they are in Rule 506 offerings, simple failures to deliver notices of certain rights to prospective investors can single-handedly result in a quick rescission of the investment being ordered by a court. The investor/promoter will have to return the principal and interest at the applicable state's post-judgment interest rate and will be liable to the plaintiff/investor for his or her attorney's fees and costs. An investor/promoter that cannot make good on a rescission order stands a greater chance of being criminally prosecuted at the end of the day.

Experienced securities counsel can minimize the risks faced by the investor/promoter by drafting disclosure documents and subscription agreements, preparing appropriate corporate records, preparing the filings with government entities, and counseling the investor/promoter on the steps required to conduct an investment solicitation that complies with applicable securities laws.

Chapter 13

A Simple Business Buyout Example

In a business buyout, state and federal broker issues, and state and federal offering statutes apply to the transaction.

Broker Licensing Issues

States have differing approaches to the sale of a business, with some holding that the sale of a business is not a securities transaction, while federal securities law and the securities laws of the other states maintain the view that a transfer of stock for value is a securities transaction.

Whether the transaction is viewed as a sale of a business or sale of a security, for compliance with federal and state law, appropriate broker licensing is necessary for any intermediaries involved in the transaction. Intermediaries are a frequent feature of the mergers and acquisition marketplace and often pose as investment bankers trying to get a percentage of a transaction that they create. In essence, these intermediaries are often no-money-down deal finders who solicit businesses with the promise of financing (that they do not have) and potential investors (from whom the capital for the transaction will be sourced) to match them up to create a financing transaction. Involving and paying brokers or other intermediaries in the transaction who are not licensed at the state or federal level can lead to a subsequent claim by the buyer or investor for rescission based upon a transaction having been conducted by unlicensed personnel. Some deals will simply collapse during the due diligence process when alert parties discover the presence of an unlicensed intermediary in the deal. Some transactions implode because an intermediary has a state license but not an appropriate federal license, and vice-versa. The type of transaction and interstate or intrastate nature of the transaction dictate the appropriate license requirements for intermediaries.

At the state level, properly-licensed intermediaries may be registered as real estate brokers or real estate agents, or as business brokers, when securities broker registration is not required by the state.

At the federal level, properly licensed financial associates typically will have at least a Series 7 (general securities representative) license issued by the Financial Industry Regulatory Authority ("FINRA"). Other appropriate FINRA or FINRA-administered licenses can include the Series 62 (corporate securities limited representative), Series 65 (uniform state securities agent), Series 79 (investment banking representative), or Series 82 (private securities offerings representative). Individuals holding current licenses can receive compensation if the merger and acquisition or capital raising transaction is encompassed within the scope of their respective license.

Raising Capital for a Business Purchase

The leveraged buyout of a small business can be achieved in several different ways in compliance with state and federal securities laws. Leaving aside the employee buyout of his or her employer, an acquisition of another company can be funded using other people's money and without the assistance of an investment banker. The goal is to raise capital from investors to finance an offer to purchase a controlling-share interest in a target company that will be owned by the deal promoter and/or his or her investors or in which the promoter will obtain the controlling shares and the target company will become obligated to repay the debt instruments held by the investors. Here is a possible scenario:

> *Bob is an investor and likes to find businesses that are undercapitalized but have an apparent niche and customer following. He tries to structure management buyout offers at a low price, participate as an executive, hire one of his turnaround specialist colleagues to run the business for up to a year, spend a significant sum on marketing, and then flip the business to a new owner for a profit. Bob has identified a software development firm that specializes in medical billing software. It has only one product but is less expensive and has fewer bells and whistles than that of the competition. It earns about $750,000 in annual revenue but is breaking even. Bob believes he can acquire the company and either enter into a joint venture with another medical software company or sell the target to a competitor. Bob needs $1,500,000 for the purchase and $250,000 for marketing, assuming he can keep the development team in place. He estimates that legal and accounting expenses may run up to $200,000 including capital raise and post-acquisition analysis of the company's accounting records. Bob believes he can flip the business for four to five million dollars within one year. Bob will seek a capital raise of two million dollars.*

Opportunity does not operate at government speed. Bob will not have the time to wait for a registered offering to clear federal or state review before he can approach the software company. Bob must conduct a private offering. Because he is seeking more than one million dollars, he qualifies for a private offering using the exemptions under Regulation D Rules 504 and 506. He will choose Rule 506(b) because he will seek only accredited investors and will want to avoid simultaneous state registration or exemption compliance, but he must already have a pre-existing relationship with the prospective investors. This is achievable because Bob has been in this business for several years and has developed a relationship with a list of prospective accredited investors, many of whom have invested with him in the past. But Bob cannot have conducted another offering within the prior twelve months or he runs the risk of being deemed to be a broker under federal law. Bob will have his legal counsel prepare an offering memorandum containing the known facts about the business and his background, and the business will offer prospective investors a convertible debenture paying a rate of return 4% above bank rates with interest payment deferred for one year. The offer to the company will be contingent on the company's cooperation during the due diligence period and Bob's ability to raise the necessary cash. Bob will cancel the offer to the company and the offering to the investors if he does not raise the two million dollars necessary to complete the offer to the company.

By offering a convertible-debt instrument to investors, Bob avoids the certainty that he will be substantially diluted by the investors' participation in the transaction, but he faces the probability that if the target company does not pay off the debt quickly the investors may convert their debt instruments into equity positions. Bob and his counsel have structured the debt instruments to minimize the dilution he will suffer and still make the offering attractive.

If Bob found a willing and cooperative target company that shares his view of its worth, this deal could work in theory because Bob has proceeded appropriately.

Chapter 14

A Simple Start-Up Business Capital Raise Example

Anytime pre-incorporation or post-incorporation, a corporation can raise capital from investors. Here is an example. XYZ Widget Corp. desires to raise one million dollars from friends, friends-of-friends, and some family members. How does it go about it?

A million dollar capital raise theoretically can be conducted in a registered offering at both the state and federal level, at the state level only, and the federal level only (if the transaction would result in the company's securities being traded on NASDAQ or similar large securities exchange), using any one of the registrations or exemptions from registration discussed above. Registration is typically expensive and slow. For example, if the board of directors of XYZ Widget Corp. engaged in a Tier I Regulation A offering ($20 million or less), it would have to undertake similar steps to conducting a SEC-reviewed, full-blown federal securities registration. This requires that the corporation prepare financial statements according to generally accepted accounting principles, have its balance sheet audited, and prepare a Regulation A Form 1-A offering circular, file it with the SEC (and the states in which investors will be sought in a Tier I offering), respond to comments from both the SEC and the states in a Tier I offering, and then publish notice about the offering in states where the offering circular has been approved for the Tier I offering. XYZ would be smart not to waste time trying to get a securities registration approved in states that require merit review because start-up companies usually will not qualify.

Tier I Regulation A offerings are not optimum for startup company capital raises. Tier II of Regulation A (offerings up to $50 million) may be attractive if the issuer expects to obtain investment from institutional investors and/or accredited investors. Regulation A offers a short six-month holding period and preempts state registration. Offers made using Regulation A will be public offerings and, because state securities registration is preempted, will avoid the small company dual state and federal registration requirement inherent in small company (non-NASDAQ) initial public offerings.

Another option is to conduct the offering under the exemption from registration provided by SEC Regulation D. Both Rule exemptions under Regulation D are available, but Rule 506(b) offerings require substantial financial disclosure to unaccredited investors, and the non-accredited investors must be knowledgeable and sophisticated about business matters. Rule 504 is available for an unlimited number of unaccredited investors but which will be coordinated with state limited offering exemptions, has a maximum capital raise of $5,000,000, and may have state investor suitability requirements. Rule 506(b) has no ceiling on the amount raised. Successive offerings are permissible so long as no more than the annual limit for each exemption is reached and that there is at least a six-month cooling-off period between offerings. Rule 506 is always preferred because state laws that pertain to offerings are preempted in a Rule 506 offering by federal law. Complying with Rule 506 removes the delay and expense caused by the state review process; however, none of these offerings can be advertised. In September 2013 Rule 506(c) went into effect, and issuers are now able to advertise their Rule 506 offerings (but can sell only to verified accredited investors).

Another option is to seek capital offshore. The corporation could conduct an offshore offering under Regulation S for which there is no dollar limit on the U.S. side, but requires that the purchasers offshore do not resell to a U.S. citizen for at least one year because securities offered under Regulation S cannot be repatriated until one year has lapsed from the start of the offering. Thought must be given to compliance with applicable foreign jurisdiction securities offering laws and regulations.

Offers can be conducted under Regulations A, D, and S simultaneously so long as the ceilings imposed by Regulation A or Rules 504 and 505 are complied with. In a more typical scenario where multiple exemptions are used, an offering could be conducted under Rule 506(b) (not advertised) and Regulation S (not advertised offshore), or using Rule 506(c) (advertised) and Regulation S (advertised, if legal in the foreign jurisdiction).

Investor crowdfunding may be an option as may be state-filed crowdfunding. However, the expenses of crowdfunding and the availability of a portal are limiting factors. Investor crowdfunding has proven to have significant portal fees that can remove more than ten percent (10%) of the proceeds raised. Also, crowdfunding portals can be picky about the issuers that they allow to conduct offerings on their platform. Portals are a business and some only want the offerings that they feel are likely to be successful to uphold the reputation of their platform. Thus, the availability of crowdfunding may be more theoretical than practical for some would-be securities issuers.

Chapter 15

CAPITAL FOR KEEPS

Keeping Investors Happy

Keeping investors happy may seem to be an improbable proposition, but attempting to do so is a primary means of avoiding litigation. Certainly, investors sue great companies and highly profitable companies all the time. Some of these suits can be characterized as being opportunistic, but others probably are the results of investor expectations not being met. How can you meet investor expectations?

I think there are four general ways to meet expectations: (1) know what the expectations are and exceed them, (2) deliver on promises, (3) communicate frequently and truthfully, and (4) continually strive to provide increased investment value. Any company that is managed with a focus on these four items may not avoid all lawsuits, but will at the least reduce their probability.

Know and Exceed Expectations. Management should always know what the expectations are in the minds of those who have entrusted them with their investment funds. Obviously, investors as a general rule expect that management will take reasonable steps designed to increase investors' returns on investment. However, I've seen many times, and to my surprise, that management takes a contemptuous view of their investors. Such managers must think that investors are hostile and greedy. There is certainly a basis in truth for that perspective, and I do not suggest that that perspective is irrational. We have a culture of litigation in this country. Private enterprise is the frequent target of governments, lawyers and class action suits, social groups, environmental groups, labor groups, politicians, news media, and the list goes on. How management treats its employees and vendors may serve as a telltale of how it will treat investors. A management culture that is growing a healthy corporation and well-run enterprise from within will almost inevitably have a beneficial outlook on the treatment of investors. A great place to work should mean that the enterprise is a great place to invest. Investors, in my view, have low expectations; so every point of contact with them that is a positive experience is likely to exceed their expectations and promote a feeling of well-being. The corporation that executes investor relations well should implicitly be inoculating itself from the prospect of avoidable negative publicity and lawsuits.

Deliver on Promises. Each person who communicates with prospective investors is personally liable under state and federal securities laws. If you promised investors something and failed to deliver on it, the broken promise is likely to be the basis for a lawsuit premised on investors' claims of reliance on your promises and their inducements to tender their funds to you. Even if you state in writing to prospective investors that you and your company are making no representations whatsoever to induce the investors to invest, you and your company continue to have an inescapable duty of good faith and fair dealing or a fiduciary duty to investors. You can execute this duty easily and effectively and within the protections of your business judgment if you keep track of what you said and then do what you said you would do or exceed it.

Frequent Truthful Communications. Public companies, for example, are required by the federal securities laws to make and disseminate current, quarterly, and annual reports of financial and other material information. All of this information is required to be truthful and accurate. By the same token, a private company that does not have legal obligations to report to the public and to the shareholder base should consider the merits of frequent truthful communications. Having a system in place that ensures that investors are receiving regular and balanced updates on the company's performance will go a long way to building up the investors' confidence in the company. Even if the news is all bad, it would be better for you and the company to be the ones who are the first to tell the story before others tell it and put their own spin on it. The truth will come out eventually anyway, whatever it is. Take the high road and disclose information that investors want to know. Don't sugarcoat the news. You are striving to be credible, and you want the investor base to be conditioned to know that it can rely on the company's version of events in good times and bad times.

Deliver Increasing Value. Most public company executives understand that one of their primary duties is to ensure that shareholder value is maximized. Private company executives need to have a similar mindset. While business cycles may make it impossible to always deliver increased earnings per share, this should always be one of private company management's goals. Again, this goes back to the understanding that when you have the control of investment funds provided by others, you need to act in their best interests ahead of your own interests or the interests of the corporation. If you have this mindset and can demonstrate the steps you take consistently to maximize shareholder value, even if you do not avoid lawsuits you'll be in a better position to defend them.

Chapter 16

PROFESSIONAL ASSISTANCE

When business is conducted on a shoestring, typically the additional expenses of accounting and legal assistance are beyond consideration. But *capital raising* on a shoestring without qualified professional assistance is foolish. Those that take money from investors, violate legal requirements, and lack the ability to return the money, face the highest probability of any group, other than those that misappropriate funds or intentionally commit fraud, of being criminally prosecuted. Jail is often the only remedy when investor money cannot be returned. As with everything else in life, there is risk and there are costs and benefits to be weighed. Not everyone goes to a doctor for an annual checkup. Not everyone takes his car for an oil change every 3,000 miles. Not everyone uses an accountant to prepare tax returns. But when raising capital, those that play fast and loose with the rules—or are completely oblivious to them—stand a good chance of facing legal action from regulators and prosecutors. All transactions have the risk that they will not work out. Eighty percent of all businesses fail in the first year. With giant odds operating against the success of an investment, it is wise to spend the time and effort to button down the offer with professional assistance to limit your legal exposure. Why risk getting sued and losing perhaps everything you have worked for? Remember, the securities laws are designed to protect the investor, not you.

Bonuses

1. Bonus Chapter (Reprinted below) from *The Secrets of Wall Street by Timothy Hogan.*
2. Sample Securities Forms (included in appendix). Securities forms are available for download at www.CapitalforKeeps.com

Bonus Chapter

"RULES OF THE GAME"[20]

Rule #1: Understand Institutional Sources. Substantial amounts of institutional equity or debt capital are generally not available for the vast majority of start-up and early-stage companies, which include most firms with less than five years of operating history and less than $5,000,000 in annual sales. Institutional equity or debt capital means capital secured primarily through professional investors, such as venture capital firms ("VCs" or "VC firms"), angel groups, family offices, private equity investment firms, retirement or pension funds, insurance companies, and capital secured through the sale of securities offered through investment banks and broker-dealers.

In the VC industry, less than 1.5% of all start-up and early-stage companies searching for capital receive their needed funding through any institutional source—on average annually, in good or bad times. In good times, generally more money is available and there is more quality deal flow. In bad times, less money is available and there is less quality deal flow. *It's all relative.* If your start-up or early-stage company is within the lucky 1.5%, the institutional equity capital source will

20 Reprinted with permission of the author of *The Secrets of Wall Street* © 2013, available at http://www.commonwealthcapital.com.

most likely control the terms of the deal and (often) demand voting control. You may have to give up substantial equity and upside participation to "seal the deal." On average, VC firms typically fund two, three, or possibly four companies out of the 1,500 (or more) deals they review each year.

"Why do most VC firms operate this way?"

They operate this way because they have no real choice—it is a matter of survival. True, more venture capital money is currently available than at any other time in history; however, the money is not being invested due to a lack of quality deal flow. In the VC industry, this reality is called "capital overhang." The VCs cannot lower their investment criteria (to fund the majority of start-up and early-stage companies) primarily because they raised capital through a prospectus to individual and institutional investors, which limits their flexibility. Specifically, they raised capital for their Funds by selling shares and setting criteria within the prospectus (their securities offering document) that limits their ability to invest in prospect companies. For example, they may have stated something like, "...the Fund will only invest in portfolio companies that are engaged in the medical supply and health care industries, nanotech as it relates to medical supplies, and surgical application or other related technologies [sector positioning limitation]; with a minimum of seven years of operating history [stage limitation]; annual sales of at least $15,000,000 [size limitation]; and the average capital commitment of $20,000,000 [capital commitment limitation]." Essentially, they pin themselves into a corner through prospectus limitation. Granted they believe that this limitation protocol mitigates portfolio risk, which it does to one degree or another—depending, of course, on how one looks at it. More importantly, however, this limiting strategy mitigates capital raising risk for the VCs. What do you think would happen if they took a prospectus with little or no limitation protocol to an institution looking to invest a couple hundred million dollars? *They would be laughed out of the room.*

"I only need $500,000. Why won't a Venture Capitalist just cut me the check?"

Unless they make a radical departure from the "old school" position and protocol of investing and managing "portfolio companies" for their Funds, it is a mathematical certainty that they will never be able to afford to simply "cut the check." Not only is it commercial suicide for a VC firm to stray from investment criteria protocol for attracting capital for their Funds, but they could not otherwise afford to manage the amounts invested in smaller companies. For instance, let's say that a VC firm was able to raise $10,000,000 in a new Fund to invest only in start-up companies. Also assume that the average amount to be invested is $500,000 per company, and that the Fund plans on investing in 20 companies this year (for diversification) with the average holding period estimated to be 5 years. After making stated investments, the Fund has 20 portfolio companies it will then need to look after. The VC firm needs to employ professional managers (in-house within the VC firm) to look after these companies. How many companies can each manager reasonably look after—2, 3, or possibly 4? Remember, the VC firm has a fiduciary duty to its shareholders of the Fund, so it cannot skimp in this area. Let us assume for this example that each manager looks after 4 companies (the high end of this estimate). In this scenario, the VC firm needs to employ 5 managers to look after all 20 portfolio companies. How much should the VC firm pay these managers in annual salaries? Should the VC pay $200,000, $250,000 or $300,000 each? Where is the line to further assure that the Fund is hiring competent managers to protect the VC firm's fiduciary duty? Let us assume that $200,000 is the line on salaries (the low end of the cost spectrum). That's 5 Managers at an annual cost of $200,000 each for a total annual cost of $1,000,000 in salaries alone. Who is going to pay for these managers' salaries? Typically, the portfolio companies need to provide immediate returns to the VC Fund to pay this cost. Most start-up companies would be hard-pressed to afford annual contributions to the VC Fund of $50,000 each year. However, let's assume that each of these portfolio companies can make annual contributions to the Fund of $50,000 each year to enable the VC Fund to afford the Managers to justify the capital invested. We do this to further define the next segment of this scenario.

After the average holding period of 5 years, the total cost of managing the investments of the Fund in these start-ups is $5,000,000 ($50,000 x 20 companies x 5 years) in salaries alone, which is now being funded by the companies within the investment portfolio. Add an extra $500,000 for other unforeseen costs, such as additional legal advisory, accounting services, etcetera, which will also be borne by the collective of all portfolio companies—for a total of $5,500,000 over that 5 year period. That's the VC Fund's overhead commitment, whether or not these companies survive to the degree that they can cover these costs. Now, the accepted truism in the industry is that 80% of these portfolio companies will fail within the first 3 years, and that 20% will succeed to a degree that should make up for the "capital losses" (and then some) of the other 80%. Thus, we can assume that out of the 20 companies funded, 16 companies (e.g., 80%) will fail—for a total capital loss of $8,000,000 of the original total Fund value of $10,000,000. If we assume that they fail during the 3rd year, then on average the 16 companies will not be able to cover 2 1/2 years of the $5,500,000 VC's overhead commitment. This equates to (16 x $50,000 x 2.5) = $2,000,000 VC overhead shortfall or loss. Let's say the VC is willing to absorb the $2,000,000 potential operating loss (note, if you knew any VCs they would laugh at that last statement), for the potential capital gains. Each of the 4 remaining portfolio companies with initial investments of $500,000 each ($2,000,000 total) would need to be liquid (publicly-traded or sold to a strategic buyer) with average values of at least $15,625,000 per company (assuming an 80% ownership interest acquired in each portfolio company by the Fund, for a $12,500,000 net value in each portfolio company to the Fund) to meet the "risk/return criteria" of 5 times the money in 5 years set by the Fund; $10,000,000 to $50,000,000—4 companies x $12,500,000 in Fund value each. *That is a far reach*. Furthermore, if you had a company with the potential to be worth $15,125,000 in 5 years, would you sell 80% of the ownership today for $500,000?

So we've made some fairly unrealistic and aggressive assumptions to entice or motivate a VC firm to adopt a business model to fund start-up or early-stage companies. First, we've asked them to demand $50,000 each year from each portfolio company; then we've asked them to shoulder an estimated $2,000,000 in internal operating losses; and lastly, we expect them to grow 4 start-up or early-stage companies, most likely each in the pre-revenue stage with an unproven business model, to a value of $15,125,000 in 5 years with only $500,000.

The point I'm trying to make here, is the math simply does not make sense for a VC firm when one assumes that the traditional VC Fund model is employed by competent managers. In addition, it does not make any sense for an entrepreneur to sell too much equity—too early and for too little—either, now does it?

You may be thinking, "*But I've read in all the trade magazines that venture capital groups are springing up all over the country and are funding deals left and right.*" Frankly, you are reading about the rare cases. Remember, the publishers of these magazines need to sell "hopes and dreams" and, ultimately, their publications. Consider the source before you jump to conclusions. They produce good stories that motivate and do have value. However, if you want to raise substantial amounts of capital while maintaining the vast majority of equity ownership and control, you should produce and execute a series of successful securities offerings to be effective in your capital raising efforts—this has more value than simply being motivated.

You could also be thinking, "*But we're different because we're being romanced by a couple of VC firms right now.*" Sorry, it is most likely a false romance. VCs must generate massive deal flow so they can "cherry pick." It costs them virtually nothing to keep you, and everyone else, hanging on. You cannot blame them—this is the nature of the industry.

All VC firms are looking to invest in the "next big thing." Yet, most of them will not know what the "next big thing" is until it is too late. That is why they have to "cherry pick" the top 1.5% of the deals they review. Nevertheless, the VC industry may need to adjust their investment criteria, or like any other industry that does not change to meet market demand...the industry may cease to exist.

Boutique investment banks and broker-dealers (specifically those with less than 100 sales representatives) are also finding it far more difficult to engage companies, at any stage of the companies' life cycles, in an investment banking securities brokerage effort. The difficulty arises in the increasing compliance burden of the SEC, Financial Industry National Regulatory Authority ("FINRA"), and North American State Securities Administrators ("NASAA). For some reason, these regulators are set out to destroy this portion of the industry. In the compliance session at a capital conference we attended in February of 2013, a former SEC enforcement attorney (on a panel of six securities attorneys) made the statement that FINRA has indicated in their internal documents that small broker-dealers are to be sought after as the primary targets for assessing fines, because they are the cause of the vast majority of the regulatory violations within the securities industry. What FINRA may fail to recognize is that the more rules they make, the more difficult it is for compliance to be met. Thus, small boutique broker-dealers may be *going the way of the dinosaurs.*

In addition, the amount of quality deal flow (e.g., companies that qualify for the investment banking relationship) is far less than it used to be and the profit margins are simply too small to make it worth it anymore. Sadly, this portion of the industry may be doomed. And in conjunction with this evolution, entrepreneurs may have no choice but to capitalize themselves "in-house" by conducting one or more securities offerings themselves.

To hedge your position and to increase the probability of success, you must compete directly with financial institutions to attract capital from individual passive investors. Keep in mind that those financial institutions need to attract capital from individual investors as well. Banks need depositors and venture capitalists need shareholders in their Funds. No matter how you look at it, it boils down to attracting individual investors; ultimately, because they *have and control the money*. Business plans and executive summaries do not meet the stringent legal requirements to raise capital from individual investors—only securities offering documents do.

Rule #2: Conduct a Series of Related Securities Offerings to Raise Capital—by Using Hybrid Securities to Maintain Voting Control and Equity Ownership. You can raise sufficient capital without giving up substantial common equity interest through the issuance of hybrid securities. This includes (but certainly is not limited to) convertible preferred stock, convertible notes, convertible bonds, non-voting common stock with married put options, participating preferred stock, notes with equity kickers, or through issuing royalty financing contracts. In the current market environment, convertible participating callable preferred stock with a high-stated dividend, a generous participation in net income, a reasonable conversion ratio into the common voting equity, and a call date that is four to five years away from the date of issue is very attractive to investors.

Selling common equity in the early stages of a company's existence generally results in selling out the company's most precious element—common equity ownership—for too little, too soon. In the world of finance, there exists what is known as "cheap" money and "expensive" money; nevertheless, it is relative and it changes. For instance, bank debt with a high interest rate seems like expensive money in the beginning; yet, if you are successful then bank debt becomes cheap money relative to selling common voting equity because it will become more valuable and, inherently, it then becomes expensive money. For example, if you borrowed $1,000,000 at a 10% interest rate for five years, that is $100,000 a year in interest or a total of $500,000. In this scenario, bank debt seems expensive. Yet, if you sold 30% of your Company's common stock for $1,000,000, and your Company is worth $5,000,000 at the end of the fifth year, that is a value of $1,500,000—or a net expense difference of $1,000,000 (the value of 30% of the Company: $1,500,000 less the $500,000 in bank interest = $1,000,000). The common stock is technically lost forever, so the net cost may be more as your Company continues to grow. *That's very expensive money.*

Now let's look at it from an investor's perspective. To reiterate the point, attempting to sell common stock in a corporation or membership/partnership ownership interest in an LLC at the early stages of a company's existence is very difficult and expensive. It is difficult because most try to sell a small amount of equity ownership for a relatively large amount of money. If there is very little cash or marketable inventory in the company, and an investor purchases 30% of the total ownership equity for $1,000,000, that investor just lost $700,000 due to dilution. An extreme dilution factor is very unattractive to any investor. In addition, if you assume success in your venture, selling any common voting equity in the early stages generally results in selling too much of your Company's most precious element—common voting equity…too soon, for too little—a critical mistake made by most entrepreneurs. There are service firms that will charge you an outrageous fee to take your start-up or early-stage company public (pink sheets or OTC bulletin board), which is one of the biggest mistakes a start-up or early-stage company can make. Repairing this mistake can be done, but for most… it is a death sentence.

If you want to control the terms of the deal and maintain the vast majority of equity ownership and voting control of your Company, while simultaneously increasing the probability of raising substantial amounts of capital, then you must conduct a series of related securities offerings using hybrid securities (that have little or no dilutive repercussions for investors) compliant with federal and state(s) securities laws, rules, and regulations. Searching for capital in any other fashion generally results in everyone attempting to change the terms of the deal, which results in lost time and lost money. Thus, the alternative becomes an extremely frustrating endeavor.

The most successful capital raising efforts are illustrated as follows:

The Basic Series of Hybrids

Seed Capital	Development Capital	Expansion Capital
Convertible Bridge Notes	Convertible Preferred Equity	Common or Preferred Equity
Amounts normally range from: $100,000 to $1,000,000	Amounts normally range from: $1,000,000 to $5,000,000	Amounts normally range from: $5,000,000+
Interest Rate Short Term Maturity DEBT CAPITAL	Stated Dividend Participating Dividend Conversion TEMPORARY EQUITY CAPITAL	Exchange Listing gives Liquidity for Acquisition Purposes
Conversion Privelage into Common Equity for Growth	Lien Position Callable	
ACTS LIKE EQUITY	ACTS LIKE DEBT	ACTS LIKE CURRENCY

1. The process begins with conducting a "Seed Capital" round, ranging from $100,000 to $1,000,000. **An ample amount of seed capital is necessary to launch a successful capital raising effort.** Seed Capital is generally raised through the issuance of one-, two-, or three-year "Seed Capital Convertible Bridge Notes" or "Convertible Participating Preferred Stock" with five-year call protection. Producing these deal structures and the related securities offering documents is relatively quick and inexpensive.
2. Seed Capital is only used to protect investor interests by (a) further protecting the company's assets (i.e., intellectual property or "IP"); (b) sustaining (not expanding) basic business operations; and (c) most importantly, hiring the right professionals to continue the process of raising capital through a series of related securities offerings with the issuance of hybrid securities in compliance with federal and state(s) securities laws.
3. A portion of the Seed Capital is used to produce and promote the next securities offering for "Development Capital." For most, Development

Capital will be sought out in the local community using the general media to solicit the securities. You can qualify for public solicitation through the general media—under SCOR, through provisions in California Securities Code (Section 1001 or 25102(n)), Regulation D Rule 506(c), or Regulation A. Because of the issuance of *convertible participating preferred equity*, Development Capital should be kept at a minimum; if one assumes success, this form of capital could get expensive due to its income participation and conversion features. Development Capital is normally used for hiring employees, especially additional management team members; capital expenditures; and (most importantly) for generating sales and increasing the revenue stream. This is easily done through "public solicitation" of the private entity's securities.

4. A portion of Development Capital is often used to produce and promote the next securities offering for "Expansion Capital" for fast growing companies. For most, Expansion Capital will be sought in the local community using the general media to solicit the securities. You can qualify for public solicitation through the general media, in the same manner as Development Capital (noted above). Additionally, Expansion Capital can be sought after in a few different ways. Due to the issuance of common equity and/or debt, Expansion Capital should be kept in balance but be sufficient to expand your Company through acquisition to increase market share and further profitability. Expansion Capital is used for expanding your Company's employee base; additional capital asset acquisitions; and other expansion plans. Under Regulation D Rule 506, you can use Expansion Capital for the acquisition of other companies and/or assets to increase revenue, reduce cumulative overhead expenses through consolidation, or both. Using the convertible participating preferred equity deal structure, one can acquire assets or entire companies by issuing a specific "series" (i.e., Series B, C, or D) of preferred equity offering directed at that acquisition. Normally, assets are acquired, thereby relieving you of the acquired company liabilities—disclosed or otherwise. In addition, by

acquiring all the assets of a company (as opposed to all the stock of a company) your Company can depreciate or amortize the acquisition, thereby reducing taxation. That preferred equity would be secured against the acquired assets, while allowing the previous owners to share in the profits of the (entire) newly created consolidated company; furthermore, they will receive a stated dividend higher than they could get elsewhere. In addition, you can create the preferred equity with a $100 per share price, and then discount it to defer capital gains taxation to the previous owners. For instance, if the negotiated purchase price of the acquired assets is $10,000,000 and the previous owners have a cost basis of $6,000,000, you could issue 100,000 shares of preferred stock at $100.00 per share. That figure equates to $10,000,000, but you would price it at $60.00 cost basis with a $40.00 of unrealized appreciation per share on your Company's, as well as the selling company's, balance sheets (accounting records), as opposed to the $100.00 per share—thereby deferring the previous owners' capital gain until they sell their newly acquired shares. By styling your securities offering in this manner, you may be able to negotiate the acquisition price to a lesser amount because of the attributes you offer in the newly created preferred equity. *Need more power in the negotiations*? Then plan on listing the preferred equity on a publicly-traded securities exchange; depending on the value of the deal, it may be worth spending the extra funds necessary for the exchange listing.

Additional Benefits of Issuing Hybrid Securities. Other significant benefits of issuing (high demand) hybrid securities include the following: (a) your common equity ownership and voting control is not diluted or lost; (b) they are in high demand, so selling them is relatively easy—preferred stock dividends may qualify for the 70-100% "dividend exclusion allowance" (essentially tax free income) for U.S. corporate investors; (c) they can be "callable", or redeemable, making this form of equity temporary (at your option) and, thus, the least expensive form of equity; (d) if these securities are listed on a publicly-traded securities exchange, offering them directly to market makers at a discount (from market price) makes raising additional rounds of capital very easy; and (e) more importantly, once listed on a publicly-traded securities exchange these securities can be used as currency for asset or company acquisition purposes (this is very important).

Note, listing "common stock" on a publicly-traded securities exchange too early is a *major mistake* for most companies. Most publicly-traded, small companies initially went public because someone "sold them" on the concept that once their common stock was traded publicly they would be able to raise capital. Although they do raise some capital, it never is what they expect; essentially, the stock becomes a penny stock. At this juncture, the trading volume dries up and the stock falls further in price due to the illiquid nature of the decrease in volume. When attempting to "float" additional common shares into the public market to raise more capital, the stock becomes further diluted as does the owners' equity interest. The securities regulators despise penny stocks, because they are fundamentally part of abusive sales tactics for "boiler room" operations. What we are proposing here is to list "hybrid securities," such as convertible notes or preferred stock. Imagine listing preferred stock on an exchange with an initial listing price of $100.00 per share. With a reasonably "high yield" through the stated dividend, you naturally stabilize that price.

Dealing with liquid securities is like turning a faucet on and off again. If you need more capital, then "float" or sell more securities—"turn it on." When your capital needs are satisfied—"turn it off." Once you understand the process of operating with publicly-traded securities, it is not difficult.

You must have ample funds (seed capital) to support the related sales and marketing efforts, whether you are selling securities privately or publicly (e.g. limited public-placements internally) or engaging in a selling effort involving a FINRA member broker-dealer. Offering $500,000 in marketing support to a FINRA member broker-dealer should get that individual's attention. If you do not have a sufficient amount of seed capital, then first raise it through a seed capital securities offering. Depending on your Company's situation, $100,000 to $300,000 of seed capital should be sufficient to obtain the larger $1,000,000 to $5,000,000 amounts of development or expansion capital.

You may be saying to yourself, "That's expensive money!"—and you'd be right. So make sure that you only attempt to engage a broker-dealer when you need to raise a serious amount of capital and your Company is producing enough cash flow that $500,000 for marketing support is not a big deal.

All "risk capital" (and all capital is "risk capital" when it involves an investment in a start-up or early-stage company), is expensive, but consider the cost of not obtaining it.

Selling securities to raise capital is like selling anything else—it takes time, money, and a concerted effort. You are simply marketing and selling an intangible asset in a highly competitive and a highly regulated environment.

There are no guarantees when it comes to raising capital, only degrees of probability. The probabilities increase in direct correlation with the amount of seed capital available to promote expanded, capital raising efforts. The more seed capital you have available, the higher the probability for a continued series of successful securities offerings. You are competing with financial institutions for individual investor funds and, therefore, you have to act like one.

In summary, consider creating hybrid securities, such as Seed Capital Convertible Bridge Notes or Participating Convertible Callable Preferred Stock (or Member Units for LLCs); develop a five-year capitalization plan, which illustrates issuing one or more of a series of these types of securities over time; and oversee the training of personnel to accomplish the task of raising the capital either "in-house" (with, or without a V.P. of Finance from the securities industry) or through a SEC registered broker-dealer, when ready. By doing so, you further assure that: 1) the capital structure does not become cost prohibitive—by implementing rolling re-financing techniques; 2) your Company maintains compliance with securities regulations and financial results are optimized; 3) you do not sell too much of your Company too early for too little; and 4) more importantly, the capital is actually raised.

Rule #3: Test the Waters. Prior to conducting a full-blown securities offering effort, one could "test the waters" by researching the local geographical area for angel investor interest, as well as their own personal market of private investor contacts, fortified with one or two prototype offering structures. This process is known as the "red herring test." **Some states do not allow for a testing of the waters through general solicitation (i.e., public media), so check with your legal counsel before you engage in this discovery activity.** To produce a "red herring" document to seek indications of interest, simply build your securities offering document and then make it a draft by including a watermark within the document that states the following: "Draft Not an Official Offering." That tactic should protect you from inadvertently making an offering of securities, where none can be made.

Still, there may be peril associated with "testing the waters." Although you may think that you are saving money by holding off on creating a final securities offering document (if indications of interest are positive), you should be prepared to sell the securities quickly. If your documents are not complete, it might take too long to finish them and investor interest may change. I prefer to *strike while the iron is hot.* If you agree, have your documents completed and ready for those who show an interest. Otherwise, it may appear that you do not really have your act together—a very bad thing when asking investors for money.

Actions to determine indications of interest are used by Wall Street firms, but you can avoid most of the formal research by shopping for high-yield investments. Act like an investor who just received $1,000,000 in a 30-year, 12% tax free municipal bond that just matured. You were getting $10,000 a month in tax-free income, and now your job is to replace that income. You are smart enough to know that you should never buy a 10-, 20-, or certainly 30-year bond in a low interest rate environment, as in the current environment. *What is out there*? Check on what the bank is offering for one-, two-, or five-year CDs. Call a stockbroker or search the Internet and find out the rates that one- to five-year corporate notes or preferred stocks are trading—based on yield. Once you complete a cursory investigation, you will know how to price your Company's securities. Just beat the yield and offer upside potential against the risk associated with your deal by designing securities that meet investor demand, and you will raise capital. [More information on pricing securities is provided in Chapter 16]

Rule #4: Create a Finance Department to Compete for Capital. If your Company is in the later-stages of development, and you are unable to engage a SEC registered broker-dealer to sell your Company's securities, consider creating an "in-house" finance department. Once you have raised sufficient seed capital or have ample cash flow from operations, a well-staffed finance department within your Company can compete with financial institutions for capital from individual investors. Staff it internally or hire someone from the securities industry with the skill set, investor contacts, and ability to raise capital exclusively for your Company. This department is headed by a Vice President (V.P.) of Finance. Working as a bona fide employee for your Company, no securities license is required. How do you find these individuals? It is relatively easy because of the securities industry's high turnover rate, especially in today's market.

Remember, only SEC registered—FINRA member broker-dealers—or bona fide employees of your Company can legally solicit and sell your Company's securities. However, you cannot pay a bona fide employee a commission from the sale of securities. The beautiful thing here is that, unlike an accountant or attorney, the V.P. of Finance is a self-funding expense with very little financial risk for your Company—if done correctly.

The reason this part of the process may seem obvious to some, but strange to others, is that most entrepreneurs come from large corporations where the company has a marketing department, a human resources department, a product production department, an operations department, and an administration department, and so on. Most large corporations have an accounting department, but it does not serve as a finance department. Normally, the financing function easily is outsourced to (or handled by) large investment or commercial banks, because the larger corporation has the where-with-all (cash flow and overall financial strength) to sustain interest and dividend payments and, therefore, inherently has less risk.

In the world of raising capital, it is well-known and accepted that hiring the right professionals (in-house or out-sourced) is truly the key to overall success. This certainly would include hiring the right accountant, attorney, and a V.P. of Finance (from the securities industry).

There are additional benefits of establishing and building an in-house finance department, such as (a) it can manage future capital raising efforts in-house or in conjunction with your SEC registered broker-dealer, as well as manage franchise operations, banking, supplier-creditor negotiations, lessee relations, product lease options, investor relations, and so on; and (b) it can function as the catalyst for an exit strategy for the owners' shares, when they are ready to divest their ownership positions. The point being, an in-house finance department is not a temporary department. On the contrary, if built correctly it can be a cornerstone of your Company.

Rule #5: Do Not Rely on Others to Raise Capital. Most entrepreneurs believe that raising capital is like selling real estate. They think that entities exist that—for a commission—will raise capital for their start-up or early-stage company. Essentially, there are—they are called SEC registered investment banks or broker-dealers, which must also be FINRA Members; however, they will not raise capital for start-up or very early-stage companies...and there are reasons why. The primary is reason is that most start-up and early-stage companies are simply too risky; history shows us that 85% of all start-up and early-stage companies fail within their first five years, primarily due to the lack of sufficient capital reserves. In addition, there's very little money in it for them because the deals are too small. If you want to pursue this route for your Company, be aware that your Company may also need to invest in marketing support (approximately $100,000 to $500,000 in additional cost) for a broker-dealer to be interested in an engagement contract with your *early- to later-stage* Company. This is not mandatory, but without it you stand very little chance of engagement. The expense associated with broker-dealer due diligence is separate. FINRA (the primary federal regulator for broker-dealers) mandates that third-party due diligence be conducted prior to broker-dealer engagement. That due diligence process can be very expensive, depending on the nature of your Company and on the dynamics of its operations. On top of those up-front, out-of-pocket expenses, you will pay a generous commission—generally 5-12% of monies raised—and, depending on the market environment, you may also give up some equity through the issuance of warrants to the broker-dealer(s). In addition, you will be doing most of the work of actually selling the securities—through the proverbial "dog and pony shows"; there is nothing like the enthusiasm of members of the company's management team to garner investor interest, and broker-dealers rely on that. This reality further justifies the hiring a V.P. of Finance...and conducting your securities offerings in-house.

WARNING! HIRING MONEY FINDERS CAN BE EXTREMELY DANGEROUS AND IT RARELY WORKS. YOU SHOULD NOT PAY ANY UP-FRONT "INVESTOR INTRODUCTORY" FEES AND YOU CANNOT PAY THEM A COMMISSION, PERFORMANCE, OR SUCCESS FEE FOR

OBTAINING CAPITAL IF AN OFFERING OF SECURITIES IS INVOLVED. IT IS YOUR RESPONSIBILITY TO COMPLY WITH FEDERAL AND STATE SECURITIES LAWS, NOT THE MONEY FINDER'S RESPONSIBILITY.

Rule #6: The Key. Raising capital for start-up and early-stage companies in any economic environment can be difficult, if not properly orchestrated. In good times, investors can expect good returns on their investment in the stock market, where the investment is easily accessible because one can sell (liquidate) their securities at any time. The resistance often lies in tying up money in an illiquid security in a private company; however, this can be overcome with the proper securities marketing and selling techniques. In bad times, investors are always waiting for good times to reappear before they make any changes in their investment portfolio. When you are competing for capital in any market environment, you simply need to compete on the basis of the following criteria:

1. Relative safety of principal;
2. Immediate return (yield); and
3. Long-term return (profit participation/capital gains).

After you have beaten the competition from a deal structuring standpoint, then you simply need to maximize the number of investors you contact—legally. As with all sales, it becomes a numbers game. In any market environment, it is far more effective to raise small amounts from many investors by being able to compete directly with financial institutions in the fixed-income securities markets with high-yield securities.

These are the fundamental techniques we have used on Wall Street and we now bring them to you on Main Street. Please read on.

About the Author

Russell C. Weigel, III, Esq.

Mr. Weigel, a Florida resident, has been practicing securities law since 1990. *Capital for Keeps* is a product of his government regulatory and private practice of law experiences.

He has continued his transactional and litigation securities practice since 2005 at his own law firm. His focus includes advising public and private company clients on capital raising transactions, preparing their SEC reports and registration statement filings, and defending clients involved in arbitrations and FINRA, SEC, and state securities enforcement matters.

From 2001 to 2005, Mr. Weigel worked successively for two law firms, in private practice, as a securities transactional and litigation attorney. He advised on public company mergers and general corporate and securities regulatory compliance matters. Mr. Weigel also defended clients involved in NYSE and SEC investigations and prosecuted and defended securities arbitration and civil litigation matters.

Between 1990 and 2001, Mr. Weigel worked for the Securities and Exchange Commission as an enforcement attorney. Mr. Weigel supervised and conducted over 80 investigations and litigated over 35 civil injunctive and administrative proceedings nationwide on behalf of the SEC, most involving allegations of fraud, sales of unregistered non-exempt securities, or regulatory compliance violations by stock promoters, public companies, broker dealers, investment advisers, and stock transfer agents, among others. Mr. Weigel also supervised investigations and litigated cases involving securities issuers' Ponzi schemes and false financial reporting.

Prior to his SEC experience, between 1989 and 1990, Mr. Weigel served the state of Florida as a criminal prosecutor.

In addition to his legal practice, Mr. Weigel serves his local community through continuous service to the Miami Rescue Mission and to his church.

Mr. Weigel is an AV-rated[21] securities attorney, a graduate of Vanderbilt University (B.A., 1986), and the University of Miami School of Law (J.D., 1989).

Mr. Weigel encourages your review of the book. Please leave a comment at www.CapitalForKeeps.com or send an e-mail to Info@CapitalForKeeps.com.

21 CV, BV, and AV are registered certification marks of Reed Elsevier Properties, Inc. in accordance with Martindale-Hubbell certification procedure's standards and policies. Martindale-Hubbell is the facilitator of a peer review process that rates lawyers. Ratings reflect the confidential opinions of members of the Bar and the Judiciary. Martindale-Hubbell ratings fall into two categories - legal ability and general ethical standards.

APPENDICES

Downloadable versions of these forms are also available at www.CapitalforKeeps.com.

Sample Form Officer and Director Questionnaire

Company throughout this questionnaire means ______________________________

NOTICE The information provided herein will be used in the preparation of documents that might or will be utilized in connection with the sale of securities and that might or will be filed with a local, state or federal agency. It must therefore be accurate, complete and true and not omit any material or important information.

QUESTIONNAIRE FOR OFFICERS, DIRECTORS AND PRINCIPAL STOCKHOLDERS

INSTRUCTIONS: Parts I and III must be completed by all persons. Part II must be completed by officers, directors, nominees for officer or director, and significant employees only. Please answer each question fully, giving the most exact and accurate answers possible as of the latest date. Attach additional pages, as necessary, and either type your answers or write legibly. Please initial the bottom of each page and sign and date the questionnaire on the final page.

PART I: General Information. (All persons must complete this section)

BACKGROUND

1. Full Name: ______________________________
(Last) (First) (Middle)

List all other names that you have used: ______________________________

____

2. Addresses:

(a) Current resident address:

____
(Street) (City) (State) (Zip Code)

(a) Other residence addresses in last ten years (include month and year):

____
(Dates) (Street) (City) (State) (Zip Code)

____

____

(c) Business address:

____
(Street) (City) (State) (Zip Code)

3. Telephone Number: (Business) ______________ (Home) ______________

4. Social Security Number: ______________________________

5. Date of Birth: ______________ Place of Birth ______________

6. If Married Spouse's:

(a) Legal name: ______________________________

(a) Social Security Number: ______________________________

(a) Place of employment: ______________________________

7. Education:

(a) Please complete:

	College or University	Field	Year Awarded
Doctorate	____________	____________	________
Masters	____________	____________	________
Licentiate	____________	____________	________
Bachelors	____________	____________	________

(a) All other colleges or universities attended:
(b) (Specify years and degrees received, if any)

(c) Specialized education:
(Provide information such as seminars, institutes, etc., giving year, subject matter other pertinent information)

(a) Professional memberships:
(b) (List all professional or other associations of which you are a member)

(a) Professional certifications:
(List all certificates awarded to you such as CPA, CPE, etc., year awarded, and state in which awarded)
(b)
(c)

SECURITY OWNERSHIP

8. Securities Owned in the Company:

(a) Do you own any stock or bonds issued by the Company?

Yes __________ No __________ If yes, please complete the following:

Type	Date of Acquisition	Consideration Given	Number of Shares or Face Amount of Bonds
____________	________	________	________
____________	________	________	________
____________	________	________	________
____________	________	________	________

(b) Do you own any option, warrants, convertible securities, stock appreciation rights or any other rights whereby you could acquire additional stock of the Company?

Yes ________ No ________ If yes, please complete the following:

Type	Number	Date of Acquisition	Exercise Price	Consideration Given	Expira-tion Date	Date of Exercise
______	______	______	______	______	______	______
______	______	______	______	______	______	______
______	______	______	______	______	______	______
______	______	______	______	______	______	______

(c) Do you participate in any plan or arrangement (other than those deferred compensation plans described in paragraph 28 below) whereby you could acquire additional stock of the Company?

Yes ________ No ________ If yes, please describe the nature of the plan, the number of shares you may acquire, and the conditions precedent, if any, to the vesting of your right:

(d) Are the securities specified in 8(a) and 8(b) held in your name? Yes ___ No ______ Do you have the sole voting and investment power over such securities: Yes ________ No ________ If not held in your name, in whose name are they held and what relationship does that person have to you? If you do not have the sole voting power over such securities, who has the voting and investment power over such securities?

(e) Does any other person (including any corporation, trust, estate or partnership) hold securities of the Company in their name for your benefit?

Yes ________ No ________ If yes, please complete the following:

Type	Name in Which Held	Date of Acquisition	Consideration Given	Number of Securities
______	______	______	______	______
______	______	______	______	______
______	______	______	______	______
______	______	______	______	______

(f) Other than as set forth in 8(a) through 8(e) above, are you, your wife, your children, or any corporation, trust, estate or partnership in which you or they have an interest entitled to any securities of the Company?

Yes ________ No ________ If yes, please complete the following:

Type	Name in Which Held	Date of Acquisition	Consideration Given	Number of Securities
________	________	________	________	________
________	________	________	________	________
________	________	________	________	________
________	________	________	________	________

9. Ownership of Other Securities:

(a) Do you have securities or other interest ownership in any other corporations or partnerships in which you are, as of the date of this questionnaire, an officer, director, principal stockholder or interest holder, or general partner? (A principal stockholder or interest holder is anyone owning 5% or more of total issued and outstanding shares or interests of the subject corporation or partnership.)

Yes __________ No _________ If yes, please complete the following:

Name and Complete Address of Corporation or Partnership	Type of Stock or Interest	Date Acquired	Consid- eration Paid	Number of Shares or Interests	Percentage Ownership of Entity
________	________	________	________	________	________
________	________	________	________	________	________
________	________	________	________	________	________
________	________	________	________	________	________

(a) Have any of the corporations, partnerships or businesses listed in 9(a) sold or issued securities of any type within the past year?

Yes __________ No _________ If yes, please give the name of the entity which sold or issued the securities, period of time in which the offering was made, the amount of the offering, present status of the entity which made the offering, your present relationship which respect to that entity and all other details known to you concerning the entity or offering.

(c) Have any of the corporations or businesses listed in 9(a) above within the past year filed a Registration Statement or Offering Statement under Regulation A with the United States Securities and Exchange Commission?

Yes __________ No _________ If yes, please describe such arrangement:

CERTAIN RELATIONSHIPS AND RELATED TRANSACTIONS

11. Transactions with Management and Others: Has there been any transaction during the Company's last fiscal year, or is there any proposed transaction, to which the Company or any subsidiary was, is, or is to be a party which you or any member of your immediate family (including your spouse, parents, children, siblings, mothers and fathers-in-laws, sons and daughters-in-law, and brothers and sisters-in-law) had, have, or will have a direct or indirect interest,

including the receipt of remuneration from the Company, but excluding those transactions which arise solely from such person's status with the Company (e.g., shareholder dividends, officer salaries, or payments to qualified persons pursuant to a company plan)?

Yes __________ No __________ If yes, please describe the transaction and state the nature and amount of such direct or indirect interest.

12. Certain Business Relationships: Are you, or have you been since the beginning of the Company's last fiscal year, an officer, Director, employee, member, associate of, of counsel to, or beneficial business or professional entity (including law firms and investment banking firms):

(a) Which has made, during the Company's last full fiscal year, or proposes to make during the Company's current fiscal year, payments to the Company or any of its subsidiaries for property or services?

Yes ______________ No __________

(b) Which the Company or any subsidiaries has made, during the Company's last fiscal year, or proposes to make during the Company's current fiscal year, payments to property or services?

Yes ______________ No __________

(c) to which the Company or any subsidiary was indebted at any time during the Company's last fiscal year?

Yes __________ No __________

(d) Specifically, a law firm which the Company has retained during the last fiscal year, or proposed to retain during the current fiscal year?

Yes __________ No __________

(e) Specifically, any investment banking firm that performed services for the registrant, other than as a participating underwriter in a syndicate; during the last fiscal year or that the registrant proposes to have performed services during the current fiscal year?

Yes __________ No __________

(f) Which has been during the last fiscal year, or proposes to be during the current fiscal year, engaged in any other relationships substantially similar in nature and scope to those relationships listed in paragraphs 12(a) to 12(e) above?

Yes __________ No __________

If the answer is "Yes" to any of the foregoing questions, please state the name of such firm, corporation, or other business or professional entity and your relationship to such entity, and described the nature and amount of the business done between the Company and such entity.

13. Indebtedness of Management: Were:

(a) you;

(a) any member of your immediate family;

(a) any corporation or organization (other than the Company or any of its subsidiaries) of which you are an executive officer or beneficial owner (direct or indirect) of 10% or more of the class of equity securities; or

(a) any trust or estate in which you have a similar beneficial interest or to which you serve as a trustee or in a similar capacity, indebted to the Company or any of its subsidiaries at any time since the beginning of the Company's last fiscal year?

Yes __________ No __________ If the answer is "Yes", please furnish the following information with respect to each such person: (a) the name of the person whose indebtedness is described above; (b) the nature of the relationship by reason of which the information is required to be given; (c) the largest aggregate amount of such indebtedness outstanding at any time since the beginning of the Company's last fiscal year; (d) the nature of the indebtedness and the transaction in which it occurred; (e) the amount of such indebtedness outstanding at present; and (f) the rate of interest paid or charged on such indebtedness.

14. Transaction with Promoters. If the Company has been organized within the past five years, have there been any transactions involving the Company and promoters? (The term "promoter" includes any person who directly or indirectly takes the initiative in founding and organizing the business of the Company and any person who, in connection with the founding and organizing the business of the Company, directly or indirectly receives in consideration of services or property, 10% or more of any class of securities of the Company or 10% or more of the proceeds from the sale of any class of such securities.)

Yes __________ No __________ If yes, please state: (a) the names of the promoters; (b) the nature and amount of anything of value received or to be received by each promoter, directly or indirectly, from the Company; and (c) the nature and amount of any assets, services, or other consideration received by the Company.

If yes, and if any assets were acquired or will be acquired by the Company from a promoter, please state: (a) the amount at which the assets were or are to be acquired; (b) the basis upon which that amount was determined; (c) the persons who made such determination and their relationship, if any, with the Company or any promoter; and (d) the price the promoter paid to acquire such assets.

15. Legal Proceedings of Company In any pending legal proceeding to which the Company, or any of its subsidiaries, is a party or to which any of its property is subject, are you or any of your associates an adverse party to, or have an interest adverse to, the Company or any of its subsidiaries:

Yes __________ No __________ If the answer "Yes", please describe the proceedings and state the nature and amount of such interest:

PART II: Management Information. (Officers, directors, and significant employees must complete this part)

16. Current Position with Company:

Director Yes __________ No __________ Since when ________________________

Officer Yes __________ No __________ Since when ________________________

What office do you hold (If any)? ____

17. Director or Officer Nominees:

(a) Have you consented to become a director of the Company?

Yes __________ (effective date: _______________) No __________

(a) Have you consented to become an officer of the Company?

Yes __________ (effective date: _______________) No __________

18. History of Employment:

(a) Please provide your employment history since graduation from college or high school or since completion of military service, including your employment, if any, with the Company.

Employer's Name, Address And Business Engaged	Duties, Position(s) and/or Office(s) Held	Exact Dates in Position Day, Month and Year From to
____________	____________	____________
____________	____________	____________
____________	____________	____________
____________	____________	____________

(b) Unless you have been employed by the Company for more than five years, please provide a brief explanation of the nature of your responsibilities in each position held during the last five years, other than positions, if any, with the Company, including the functions you performed in each position and, when applicable, the number of persons you supervised:

____

____

____

____

19. Employment with Affiliates. Have you during the past five years been or are you now, employed, including as an officer or director, by a subsidiary, parent, or affiliate of the Company?

Yes __________ No __________ If the answer is yes, name the company and state the nature and term of your employment:

20. Directorships. Are you the director of any other company which has a class as securities that are publicly treaded or registered under the Securities Exchange Act of 1934, or, are you a director of any company registered as an investment company under the Investment Company Act of 1940?

Yes __________ No __________ If yes, please state the following:

Company's Full Name and Address	Dates of Directorship From to

21. Certain Agreements. Were you selected as an officer or director of the company pursuant to any arrangement or understanding between you and any other person?

Yes __________ No __________ If yes, what was such arrangement or understanding?

22. Family Relationships. Is there any family relationships by blood, marriage, or adoption, not more remotely first cousin, between you and any other officer or director, or any person nominated or chosen to become an officer or director, of the Company or any of its subsidiaries?

Yes __________ No __________ If yes, what are such relationships and what are such persons' names?

23. Certain Relationships and Interests. Do you or your affiliates have, or propose to have, any of the following relationships or interests in or with the Company, including its subsidiaries?

(a)	Manufacturer for Company	Yes __________	No __________
(b)	Supplier to Company	Yes __________	No __________
(c)	Customer of Company	Yes __________	No __________
(d)	Service Agent for Company	Yes __________	No __________
(e)	Contractor with Company	Yes __________	No __________
(f)	Real estate contract with Company	Yes __________	No __________
(g)	Company car use, plan use, credit card use	Yes __________	No __________
(h)	Loans to or from Company	Yes __________	No __________
(i)	Assignment of personal interests property,		
(ii)	rights, patents, trademarks, etc. to Company	Yes __________	No __________
(j)	Company pays private club dues	Yes __________	No __________
(k)	Company pays for repairs to personal property	Yes __________	No __________
(l)	Company reimburses expenses incurred for		
(m)	Non-business items	Yes __________	No __________
(m)	Company pays for any insurance	Yes __________	No __________
(n)	Use of Company's outside professional advisors		
	For personal advice at the Company's cost	Yes __________	No __________
(o)	Insurance	Yes __________	No __________
(p)	Company death benefits whereby wife or		
(q)	Children hold stock or other interest	Yes __________	No __________

(r) Special compensation or remunerations
(s) From Company Yes __________ No __________
(r) Company guarantees on personal loans, indebtedness, etc. Yes __________ No __________
(s) Company owns apartment, house, or Residence for personal use Yes __________ No __________
(s) Voting trust, stock cross purchase agreements, First right of refusal agreements, irrevocable Proxies, secret controls, or other controlling Measures with other shareholders, directors or officers of Company Yes __________ No __________
(u) Interest in other companies, actually or proposed to be acquired, merged or consolidated with Company Yes __________ No __________
(v) Power of appointment over other officers or Directors Yes __________ No __________
(w) Professional or family relationship, including
(x) as bank or banker, lending institution, savings
(y) and loan association, insurance company,
(z) broker-dealer, underwriter, or company counsel
(aa) with the Company Yes __________ No __________
(bb) Proposed contracts, personal or otherwise, with Company Yes __________ No __________
(w) Family or other relationship with Company
(x) Auditors Yes __________ No __________
(y) Positions as officer or director held by family
(z) Members Yes __________ No __________
(aa) Lease, participation, or joint venture arrangements
(bb) With the Company Yes __________ No __________
(bb) Corporate opportunities not afforded Company Yes __________ No __________
(cc) Litigation by or against Company or by or against any officer or director Yes __________ No __________
(dd) Interest in any employment contract, in force
(ee) Or terminated Yes __________ No __________
(ee) Conflicts of interest Yes __________ No __________
(ff) Finder's fee arrangement on Company business Yes__________ No __________
(gg) Licensor or licensee of the Company Yes __________ No __________
(hh) Consultant to the Company Yes __________ No __________
(ii) Guarantor of Company's debts Yes__________ No __________
(jj) Purchaser from or seller to the Company Yes__________ No __________

If "Yes" to any of the above, please provide details, including where appropriate, the portion which is properly attributable to Company business vs. personal business.

24. Competition:

(a) Do you or any firm, person, corporation, or entity in which you have an interest compete with (or have an interest in) the Company?

Yes __________ No __________ If yes, please identify:

(b) Will you or any firm, person, corporation or entity in which you have an interest compete directly or indirectly in the future with the Company?

Yes __________ No __________ If yes, please identify:

(c) Are you or any firm, person, corporation or entity in which you have an interest engaged in the same general type of business as the Company is or intends to engage:

Yes __________ No __________ If yes, please identify:

(d) Are you subject to any noncompetition agreements?

Yes __________ No __________ If yes, please describe:

25. Certain Affiliations:

(a) Have you ever been or are you now an officer, director, promoter, or principal stockholder of a public company, or an affiliate of a broker-dealer or underwriter which was or is subject to a Suspension of a Regulation A or a "Stop Order" on a Registration Statement, or a "Cease and Desist" order from any state?

Yes __________ No __________ If yes, provide full details:

(a) Have you ever had, or have you ever been affiliated with any entity that has had a license or registration as legal counsel or as a securities dealer, broker, salesman, or investment advisor denied, suspended or revoked or have you or any entity with which you were affiliated ever been suspended or expelled from membership in any securities exchange or association of securities dealers or investment advisors?

Yes __________ No __________ If yes, provide full details:

(c) Do you or any member of your family have any direct or indirect affiliation or association as an officer, director, general partner, employee or agent with any member firm of the National Association of Securities Dealers, Inc. Or any other broker, bank, savings and loan institution, insurance company, registered investment company, registered investment advisory firm, or any similar institutional-type investor:

Yes __________ No __________ If yes, describe their position and the extent to which, if any, they may influence the buying or selling of securities by any such entity:

26. Past Compensation. Was any remuneration paid or distributed to you or accrued for your account for services in any capacity to the Company or its subsidiaries during the Company's last fiscal year in the form of:

(a) Salaries, fees, commissions, bonuses, securities or property?

Yes __________ No __________ If Yes, list all such remuneration:

Type of Compensation	Amount Received

(b) coverage by any life insurance, health insurance or medical reimbursement plan of the Company or its subsidiaries?

Yes __________ No __________ If yes, list all such remuneration:

Type of Plan	Is the Plan Generally Available To Salaried Employees?	Any Amounts Received or Accrued to your Account

_____________________ Yes ________ No ________ Yes __ No ________

_____________________ Yes ________ No ________ Yes __ No ________

_____________________ Yes ________ No ________ Yes __ No ________

(c) personal benefits received directly or indirectly from the Company and its subsidiaries:

Yes ________ No ________ If yes, describe all such remuneration:

(d) other, including contingent, forms of remunerations:

27. Current Compensation. Is any remuneration proposed to be paid to you for services in any capacity to the Company or its subsidiaries in the Company's current fiscal year in the form of:

(a) Salaries, fees, commissions, bonuses, securities or property?

Yes ________ No ________ If yes, list all such remuneration:

Type of Compensation	Amount Received

(b) Coverage by any life insurance, health insurance or medical reimbursement plan of the Company or its subsidiaries?

Yes ________ No ________ If yes, list all such remuneration:

Type of Plan	To Salaried Employees?	Accrued to Your Account
	Yes ________ No ________	Yes ________ No ________
	Yes ________ No ________	Yes ________ No ________
	Yes ________ No ________	Yes ________ No ________
	Yes ________ No ________	Yes ________ No ________

(c) Personal benefits received directly or indirectly from the Company and its subsidiaries:

Yes ________ No ________ If yes, describe all such remuneration:

(d) Contingent forms of remuneration, including proposed compensation plans?

Yes ________ No ________ If yes, describe all such remuneration

28. Stock Option and Stock Appreciation Right Plans. During the Company's last fiscal year, did you acquire or exercise any options, warrants, convertible securities, rights, bonuses, stock appreciation rights or other forms of deferred compensation from Company?

Yes __________ No __________ If yes, please complete the following:

Type	Date of Acquisition	Exercise Price	Consideration Given	Number of Securities	Expiration Date	Date of Exercise
________	__________	_______	_________	________	________	_______
________	__________	_______	_________	________	________	_______
________	__________	_______	_________	________	________	_______
________	__________	_______	_________	________	________	_______

29. Compensation of Directors. If you are a director of the Company:

(a) State any standard compensation for your services, including the amount, (e.g., $100 per meeting attended):

None _________ Or ____

(a) State any additional amounts payable for committee participation or special assignments:

None _________ Or ____

(c) describe any other arrangement whereby, during the Company's last fiscal year, you received compensation from the Company for services as a director, stating amounts paid:

None _________ Or ____

30. Change of Control and Termination of Employment Arrangements: Are there any compensatory plans or arrangements, including payments to be received from the Company, associated with a change of control of the Company or associated with your resignation, retirement or any other termination of your employment with the Company, or its subsidiaries, including any pension, profit sharing, or retirement plans, annuities or employment contracts?

Yes __________ No __________ If yes, describe the plan, including amounts to be paid:

LEGAL PROCEEDINGS

31. Involvement in Certain Legal Proceedings. During the past five years:

(a) was a petition under the federal bankruptcy laws or any state insolvency law filed by or against, or was a receiver, fiscal agent, or similar officer appointed by a court for the business or property of, you, any partnership in which you were a general partner at or within two years before the time of such filing or appointment, or any corporation or business association of which you were an executive officer at or within two years before the time of such filing or appointment?

Yes __________ No __________

(b) were you convicted in a criminal proceeding or are you the subject of any presently pending criminal proceeding (excluding traffic violations and other minor offenses)?

Yes___________ No __________

(c) were you the subject of any order, judgment, or decree, not subsequently reversed, suspended, or vacated, of any court of competent jurisdiction which permanently or temporarily enjoined you from, or otherwise limited the following activities:

(i) Acting as an investment advisor, underwriter, broker or dealer in securities, or as an affiliated person, director or employee of any investment company, bank, savings and loan association, or insurance company, or engaging in or continuing any conduct or practice in connection with such activity?
Yes ___________ No ____________

(ii) Engaging in any type of business?

Yes ___________ No ____________

(iii) engaging in any activity in connection with the purchase or sale of any security or in connection with any violation of federal or state securities laws?

Yes __________ No __________

(d) were you the subject of any order, judgment, or decree, not subsequently reversed, suspended or vacated, of any federal or state authority barring, suspending, or otherwise limiting for more than 60 days your right to engage in any activity described in subparagraph 31(c) above or to be associated with persons engaged in any such activity?
Yes __________ No __________

(e) were you found by a court of competent jurisdiction in a civil action, or by the Securities and Exchange Commission, to have violated any federal or state securities law, and the judgment in such civil action, or finding by the Securities and Exchange Commission, has not been subsequently reversed, suspended, or vacated:

Yes __________ No __________

If the answer if "Yes" to any of the foregoing questions, please describe such event or events, and give the following information: case number, dates, defendant's name, the name of the court and its jurisdiction, allegations, disposition, and other pertinent information.

32. Other Legal Proceedings:

(a) Have you ever been involved in any fraud litigation:

Yes __________ No __________

Federal Securities Laws Yes__________ No __________
State Securities Laws Yes __________ No __________
Other Yes __________ No __________

If your answer is "Yes" to any of the foregoing questions, please describe such event or events, and give the following information: case number, dates, defendant's name, the name of the court and its jurisdiction, allegations, disposition, and other pertinent information:

(b) Are there any judgments outstanding against you?

Yes __________ No __________

Nature of Judgment	Amount	Name of Court	City and State of Court

(c) Have you or any corporation or partnership which you control, are affiliated with, or were affiliated with ever been involved in any litigation or proceedings with any governmental or other entity?

Yes __________ No __________ If yes, please provide full details:

33. Other Material Information

(a) In the last ten years, have you ever been terminated from any employment position?

If yes, please state whether or not the termination was for cause and describe the circumstances surrounding the termination.

(b) Is there any other situation, circumstance, or matter not disclosed above but which you believe might be something your attorney would want to know if asked? If so, please describe.

PART III: Signature. (All persons must complete.)

33. Other Material Information. Is there any other fact, incident, event, circumstance, condition, or situation not covered above which relates to you and which may be considered material in describing your background and your current and future relationship with the Company?

Yes __________ No __________ If so, please provide details

34. Representations and Warranties:

The undersigned has prepared and carefully read the above representations. The undersigned understands that:

(a) the Company, the underwriter (if applicable), and their attorneys will rely upon the representations made above when preparing or reviewing documents to be filed with the United Securities and Exchange Commission and other governmental agencies.

(a) one who causes documents to be misleading may be held liable civilly to investors and other persons who are damaged as a result of such misrepresentation.

In view of the situation described above, the undersigned represents that:

(a) I have considered carefully each of the above representations;

(a) I have answered each question fully; and

(a) I have knowledge of no facts other than as set forth above, which might be construed to qualify any of the above representations.

I represent that if any change occurs with respect to any of the above representations, I will report such change to the Company, the Underwriter (if applicable), and their attorneys.

____________________________ ___________________________________

Date Signature

STATE OF }
} **SS:**
COUNTY OF }

Sworn to and subscribed before me this ________ day of ______________, 2014, by ______________________. He/She personally appeared before me at the time of this notarization.

He/She is:

Personally Known to me ________ OR

Produced Identification ________

Type of Identification Produced: _____________________.

____

Notary Public [signature]

____

[print name]

State of ____________________

Commission No.:_____________

Sample Due Diligence Checklist
DUE DILIGENCE CHECKLIST

I. ORGANIZATIONAL MATERIALS AND CORPORATE MATTERS

1. Articles of Incorporation and bylaws and all amendments thereto or restatements thereof of the Company (including predecessor), subsidiaries and affiliates, or any limited liability company agreement, limited partnership agreement, or equivalent governing documents.
2. A schedule of the Company's locations.
3. List of jurisdictions where the Company or its subsidiaries have substantial contacts; list of jurisdictions in which the Company or its subsidiaries are qualified to do business and evidence of such qualification; pending applications of the Company to register as a foreign corporation in any state in which the Company is not currently qualified to do business.
4. List of subsidiaries, affiliates and minority holdings of the Company.
5. The Company's minute book including all minutes of all meetings of the shareholders, Board of Directors and committees of the Board of Directors of the Company, its subsidiaries and affiliates since inception (including written consents in lieu of meetings and all notices/waivers of notice).
6. List of Board of Directors committees of the Company, its subsidiaries and affiliates.
7. Shareholder records of the Company, its subsidiaries and affiliates.
8. Stock purchase and repurchase agreements.
9. Copies of agreements relating to rights of first refusal and options.
10. Stock restriction agreements.
11. Warrants, Warrant Agreements and other rights to subscribe for securities.
12. Specimen copies of all classes of stock and debt certificates.
13. Voting agreements, voting trusts, proxies etc.
14. Registration rights agreements.
15. Stockholder's agreements.

16. A Certificate of Good Standing from the Secretary of State of the state where the Company is formed.
17. Copies of all applicable lease agreements for all Company offices, warehouse space, or other locations.
18. All press releases issued by the Company since inception.

II. SALES OF SECURITIES OF THE COMPANY, SUBSIDIARIES AND AFFILIATES

1. Documents relating to private placements of securities, including documentation regarding exemptions from, or registrations under, the federal and state securities laws, including the private placement memoranda, investor questionnaires, subscription agreements, proof of purchase of each investment, copy of Form D filed for the transaction and proof of compliance with state law Rule 506 notice filing and fee requirements.
2. List of 5% shareholders of the Company, as well as a complete shareholder list.
3. Documents relating to any future sales of securities.
4. Board resolution approving and authorizing the capital raise and delegating authority to certain officers to prepare documents.
5. Copies of all resolutions approving prior equity or debt issuances.
6. Copies of all evidence of prior securities sales.

III. BACKGROUND MATERIALS

1. Reports or significant news or magazine stories on the Company, its subsidiaries or affiliates since inception.
2. Federal, State, and foreign tax returns for the Company, its subsidiaries and affiliates, if any, for the past 3 years.
3. Description of any federal, state, local or foreign audits or correspondence from tax authorities.
4. Copies of any tax settlement documents from the IRS from the prior three years.
5. Copies of all employment tax filings from the past three years.
6. Copies of any tax liens.
7. Copies of any tax opinion.

8. Identify and collect documentary support for the MD&A discussion of known trends pertaining to liquidity, capital resources, and results of operations. Disclosure of information that can affect revenues can and should include knowledge of product failures and limitations, where applicable.
9. All available information about competitors.

IV. HUMAN CAPITAL

1. Management and employee contracts.
    a. Employment, consulting, compensation, confidentiality and non-compete agreements with any employees or independent contractors.
    b. Employee manual or handbook of policies.
    c. Collective bargaining or other labor agreements, including any side letters and union contracts of the Company, its subsidiaries or affiliates.
    d. Insurance contracts (e.g., life, disability, etc.) on any employee.
    e. List of officers and other key personnel and their salaries, indicating the percentages of their time estimated to be devoted to the Company's business if they are less than full-time employees of the Company.
2. Company organization chart.
3. A list of employees including titles and salaries, and total number of employees in marketing, sales, administration, etc.
4. A description of all employee litigation, claims and disputes as well as labor disputes within the last three years.
5. Benefit and Option Plans.
    a. All incentive stock option plans and forms of agreements, and amendments thereto.
    b. All non-qualified stock option plans and forms of agreements, and amendments thereto.
    c. List of option grants, indicating names of grantees, options exercised and options outstanding.
    d. 401(K) savings and retirement plan, and amendments thereto.

e. Other stock option, deferred compensation, equity participation, profit sharing, bonus, pension, medical, retirement, welfare or other employee benefit plans, if any.

VI. SIGNIFICANT CONTRACTUAL OBLIGATIONS OF THE COMPANY, SUBSIDIARIES AND AFFILIATES

1. Leases.
    a. All real estate leases.
    b. All equipment leases.
2. Customer Agreements.
    a. List of customers accounting for over 10% of revenues and amount and percentage of revenues for each fiscal year for the past five years.
    b. The Company's customer list, indicating the amount of sales to each customer.
3. A list of all products or services.
4. Copies of the Company's standard terms and conditions and samples of invoices.
5. Copies of all complaints or warranty claims.
6. Supplier Agreements.
    a. Agreements with suppliers of goods, services, equipment and raw materials (contracts, purchase orders, etc.) (including contract manufacturers, raw materials brokers, contract laboratories, domestic and foreign).
    b. List of suppliers accounting for over 10% of product supply, and dollar amount and percentage of purchases.
    c. Documents relating to manufacturing and distribution arrangements.
7. Sales rep agreements.
8. Loan Documents.
    a. Documents relating to any lines of credit on which the Company is obligated (line of credit, note, security agreement, etc.).
    b. Mortgages on Company-owned facilities.
    c. Documents relating to any lines of credit on which the Company is obligated (including proposed future borrowings).
    d. Documents relating to capital lease obligations.

   e. Any other loan agreements.
9. Contracts between the Company, subsidiaries and affiliates.
10. Insurance policies or summary of coverage from insurance agent or broker property, liability, life, directors and officers indemnification, business interruption, property title, etc.
11. Foreign Revenues.
   a. Any documents in connection with sales in foreign countries.
   b. Schedule of non-U.S. revenues by amount and percentage.
   c. Schedule listing all non-U.S. facilities and employees.
12. Information on Backlog.
13. All material contracts or commitments other than as covered above.

VII. MATERIAL PROPERTY AND ASSETS

1. Deeds and titles to any property owned outright.
2. List of bank accounts.
3. Documents relating to any encumbrances on any property owned outright.
4. Contracts related to construction of facilities, if any.
5. Any recent title or appraisal report with respect to material properties and assets.
6. Results from recent U.C.C. searches.
7. Copies of all U.C.C. filings.
8. A schedule of documents relating to any sales or leases to another party of any Company property, plant or equipment in the prior three years.
9. Copies of all copyright applications and approvals, trademark applications and approvals, and patent applications and approvals.
10. Schedule and summary of any intellectual property records.

VII. ACCOUNTING, LEGAL, ADMINISTRATIVE AND REGULATORY MATTERS

1. Financial statements of the Company, its subsidiaries and affiliates for all fiscal years since inception.
2. Auditor's prior year comment letter issued to management.
3. The Company's general ledger.
4. A schedule of all debt and contingent liabilities.

5. An inventory schedule.
6. Accounts receivable and accounts payable schedules.
7. Copies of any business or asset valuations.
8. A schedule of domestic and foreign patents, trademarks, copyrights and applications.
9. A description of know-how and other unregistered intellectual property.
10. Copies of all consulting agreements, work for hire agreements, licenses, and any assignments of intellectual property.
11. Any documents relating to material write-downs or write-offs of notes or accounts receivable other than in the ordinary course of business.
12. A list of any claims by or against the Company regarding intellectual property.
13. Copies of any governmental licenses, permits, or consents.
14. A description of the Company's marketing plans, budgets, and printed marketing materials.
15. Copies of all insurance policies, including general liability, product liability, errors and omissions, directors and officers, personal and real property, worker's compensation, title insurance, and other insurance.
16. A schedule of the insurance claims history over the prior three years.
17. Accountants' reports and management letters from auditors to the Company and/or its Board of Directors for the last five years.
18. All letters from the Company to the Company's independent public accountants for the past five years regarding certain representations requested by the Company's independent public accountants in connection with their audits of the Company.
19. A list and summary of all threatened or pending litigation matters (and additional information concerning pending litigation and any investigations or proceedings by any governmental agency), including copies of all pleadings, court rulings, etc.
20. Royalty or license agreements.
21. Documentation (including all necessary permits) relating to governmental or environmental matters, including hazardous substances.

22. All filings, reports, registration statements, correspondence, complaints, consent decrees, determination orders, etc., relating to federal regulatory agencies, and all state local agencies performing similar functions, including but limited to:
    a. Securities and Exchange Commission (i.e. reports on Form 10-K, 10-Q, 8-K, copies of all registration statements filed by the Company or its predecessor, etc.)
    b. Environmental Protection Agency.
    c. Copies of any environmental audits.
    d. A list of hazardous substances used or handled by the Company.
    e. Copies of all environmental permits and licenses.
    f. A list of any environmental litigation or investigations.
    g. Equal Employment Opportunity Commission.
    h. Occupational Safety and Health Administration.
    i. Internal Revenue Service and state revenue departments, including all federal and state tax returns filed since inception and the results of any IRS audit or inquiries.
    j. Health and Human Services.
    k. Other (e.g., Department of State, Department of Justice, Federal Trade Commission, Department of Labor, Department of Commerce).
    l. Any other Federal, State or local regulatory agencies applicable to the Company's business.
    m. Schedule of government licenses, permits, permissions, approvals and the like, including under local zoning and other land-use regulations.
23. All correspondence and documents relating to material contingent liabilities.

VIII. DIRECTORS AND OFFICERS OF THE COMPANY

1. Director and officer questionnaires if requested.
2. Officer or director loans or guarantees to or from the Company or any related entity.
3. All documentation on related party transactions since inception.

4. All contracts or agreements with or pertaining to the Company and to which directors, officers or owners of more than 5% of the stock of the Company or their affiliates are parties.
5. Any documents relating to any other transactions between the Company and any director, officer or owner of more than 5% of the stock of the Company or their affiliates.
6. All documents pertaining to any receivables from or payables to directors, officers or owners of more than 5% of the stock of the Company or their affiliates.

IX. MISCELLANEOUS

1. Documents relating to any future facilities expansion or acquisitions.
2. Schedule of sales and income as a percentage of total sales and income for last three fiscal years.
3. Correspondence and documentation pertaining to potential mergers or acquisitions by the Company, its subsidiaries and affiliates, whether or not definitive, binding or consummated.
4. Internal financial budgets and projections and business plans, capital expenditure budgets, and reviews of or comparisons with actual results for evaluation of current projections.

Any other documents or Information which, in your judgment, are significant with respect to any portion of the business of the Company or which should be considered and reviewed in making disclosures regarding the business and financial condition of the Company.

Sample SEC Form D

FORM D
Notice of Exempt Offering of Securities

U.S. Securities and Exchange Commission
Washington, DC 20549
(See instructions beginning on page 5)

OMB APPROVAL
OMB Number: 3235-0076
Expires: September 30, 2016
Estimated average burden hours per response: 4.00

Intentional misstatements or omissions of fact constitute federal criminal violations. See 18 U.S.C. 1001.

Item 1. Issuer's Identity

Name of Issuer

Previous Name(s) ☐ None

Entity Type (Select one)
- ☐ Corporation
- ☐ Limited Partnership
- ☐ Limited Liability Company
- ☐ General Partnership
- ☐ Business Trust
- ☐ Other (Specify)

Jurisdiction of Incorporation/Organization

Year of Incorporation/Organization
(Select one)
○ Over Five Years Ago ○ Within Last Five Years (specify year) ○ Yet to Be Formed

(If more than one issuer is filing this notice, check this box ☐ and identify additional issuer(s) by attaching Items 1 and 2 Continuation Page(s).)

Item 2. Principal Place of Business and Contact Information

Street Address 1 | Street Address 2

City | State/Province/Country | ZIP/Postal Code | Phone No.

Item 3. Related Persons

Last Name | First Name | Middle Name

Street Address 1 | Street Address 2

City | State/Province/Country | ZIP/Postal Code

Relationship(s): ☐ Executive Officer ☐ Director ☐ Promoter

Clarification of Response (if necessary)

(Identify additional related persons by checking this box ☐ and attaching Item 3 Continuation Page(s).)

Item 4. Industry Group (Select one)

○ **Agriculture**

Banking and Financial Services
- ○ Commercial Banking
- ○ Insurance
- ○ Investing
- ○ Investment Banking
- ○ Pooled Investment Fund

If selecting this industry group, also select one fund type below and answer the question below:
- ○ Hedge Fund
- ○ Private Equity Fund
- ○ Venture Capital Fund
- ○ Other Investment Fund

Is the issuer registered as an investment company under the Investment Company Act of 1940? ○ Yes ○ No

- ○ Other Banking & Financial Services

○ **Business Services**

Energy
- ○ Electric Utilities
- ○ Energy Conservation
- ○ Coal Mining
- ○ Environmental Services
- ○ Oil & Gas
- ○ Other Energy

Health Care
- ○ Biotechnology
- ○ Health Insurance
- ○ Hospitals & Physicians
- ○ Pharmaceuticals
- ○ Other Health Care

○ **Manufacturing**

Real Estate
- ○ Commercial
- ○ Construction
- ○ REITS & Finance
- ○ Residential
- ○ Other Real Estate

○ **Retailing**

○ **Restaurants**

Technology
- ○ Computers
- ○ Telecommunications
- ○ Other Technology

Travel
- ○ Airlines & Airports
- ○ Lodging & Conventions
- ○ Tourism & Travel Services
- ○ Other Travel

○ **Other**

SEC1972 (9/13) Form D 1

FORM D

U.S. Securities and Exchange Commission
Washington, DC 20549

Item 5. Issuer Size (Select one)

Revenue Range (for issuer not specifying "hedge" or "other investment" fund in Item 4 above)

- No Revenues
- $1 - $1,000,000
- $1,000,001 - $5,000,000
- $5,000,001 - $25,000,000
- $25,000,001 - $100,000,000
- Over $100,000,000
- Decline to Disclose
- Not Applicable

OR

Aggregate Net Asset Value Range (for issuer specifying "hedge" or "other investment" fund in Item 4 above)

- No Aggregate Net Asset Value
- $1 - $5,000,000
- $5,000,001 - $25,000,000
- $25,000,001 - $50,000,000
- $50,000,001 - $100,000,000
- Over $100,000,000
- Decline to Disclose
- Not Applicable

Item 6. Federal Exemptions and Exclusions Claimed (Select all that apply)

- Rule 504(b)(1) (not (i), (ii) or (iii))
- Rule 504(b)(1)(i)
- Rule 504(b)(1)(ii)
- Rule 504(b)(1)(iii)
- Rule 505
- Rule 506(b)
- Rule 506(c)
- Securities Act Section 4(a)(5)

Investment Company Act Section 3(c)

- Section 3(c)(1)
- Section 3(c)(2)
- Section 3(c)(3)
- Section 3(c)(4)
- Section 3(c)(5)
- Section 3(c)(6)
- Section 3(c)(7)
- Section 3(c)(9)
- Section 3(c)(10)
- Section 3(c)(11)
- Section 3(c)(12)
- Section 3(c)(13)
- Section 3(c)(14)

Item 7. Type of Filing

New Notice **OR** Amendment

Date of First Sale in this Offering: ________ **OR** First Sale Yet to Occur

Item 8. Duration of Offering

Does the issuer intend this offering to last more than one year? Yes No

Item 9. Type(s) of Securities Offered (Select all that apply)

- Equity
- Debt
- Option, Warrant or Other Right to Acquire Another Security
- Security to be Acquired Upon Exercise of Option, Warrant or Other Right to Acquire Security
- Pooled Investment Fund Interests
- Tenant-in-Common Securities
- Mineral Property Securities
- Other (describe)

Item 10. Business Combination Transaction

Is this offering being made in connection with a business combination transaction, such as a merger, acquisition or exchange offer? Yes No

Clarification of Response (if necessary)

FORM D U.S. Securities and Exchange Commission
Washington, DC 20549

Item 11. Minimum Investment

Minimum investment accepted from any outside investor $ ☐

Item 12. Sales Compensation

Recipient ☐
Recipient CRD Number ☐ ☐ No CRD Number

(Associated) Broker or Dealer ☐ ☐ None
(Associated) Broker or Dealer CRD Number ☐ ☐ No CRD Number

Street Address 1 ☐
Street Address 2 ☐

City ☐
State/Province/Country ☐
ZIP/Postal Code ☐

States of Solicitation ☐ All States

☐ AL ☐ AK ☐ AZ ☐ AR ☐ CA ☐ CO ☐ CT ☐ DE ☐ DC ☐ FL ☐ GA ☐ HI ☐ ID
☐ IL ☐ IN ☐ IA ☐ KS ☐ KY ☐ LA ☐ ME ☐ MD ☐ MA ☐ MI ☐ MN ☐ MS ☐ MO
☐ MT ☐ NE ☐ NV ☐ NH ☐ NJ ☐ NM ☐ NY ☐ NC ☐ ND ☐ OH ☐ OK ☐ OR ☐ PA
☐ RI ☐ SC ☐ SD ☐ TN ☐ TX ☐ UT ☐ VT ☐ VA ☐ WA ☐ WV ☐ WI ☐ WY ☐ PR

(Identify additional person(s) being paid compensation by checking this box ☐ and attaching Item 12 Continuation Page(s).)

Item 13. Offering and Sales Amounts

(a) Total Offering Amount $ ☐ **OR** ☐ Indefinite

(b) Total Amount Sold $ ☐

(c) Total Remaining to be Sold $ ☐ **OR** ☐ Indefinite
(Subtract (a) from (b))

Clarification of Response (if necessary)

☐

Item 14. Investors

Check this box ☐ if securities in the offering have been or may be sold to persons who do not qualify as accredited investors, and enter the number of such non-accredited investors who already have invested in the offering: ☐

Enter the total number of investors who already have invested in the offering: ☐

Item 15. Sales Commissions and Finders' Fees Expenses

Provide separately the amounts of sales commissions and finders' fees expenses, if any. If an amount is not known, provide an estimate and check the box next to the amount.

Sales Commissions $ ☐ ☐ Estimate

Finders' Fees $ ☐ ☐ Estimate

Clarification of Response (if necessary)

☐

FORM D U.S. Securities and Exchange Commission

Washington, DC 20549

Item 16. Use of Proceeds

Provide the amount of the gross proceeds of the offering that has been or is proposed to be used for payments to any of the persons required to be named as executive officers, directors or promoters in response to Item 3 above. If the amount is unknown, provide an estimate and check the box next to the amount. $ ☐ Estimate

Clarification of Response (if necessary)

Signature and Submission

Please verify the information you have entered and review the Terms of Submission below before signing and submitting this notice.

Terms of Submission. In Submitting this notice, each identified issuer is:

Notifying the SEC and/or each State in which this notice is filed of the offering of securities described and undertaking to furnish them, upon written request, in accordance with applicable law, the information furnished to offerees.*

Irrevocably appointing each of the Secretary of the SEC and the Securities Administrator or other legally designated officer of the State in which the issuer maintains its principal place of business and any State in which this notice is filed, as its agents for service of process, and agreeing that these persons may accept service on its behalf, of any notice, process or pleading, and further agreeing that such service may be made by registered or certified mail, in any Federal or state action, administrative proceeding, or arbitration brought against the issuer in any place subject to the jurisdiction of the United States, if the action, proceeding or arbitration (a) arises out of any activity in connection with the offering of securities that is the subject of this notice, and (b) is founded, directly or indirectly, upon the provisions of: (i) the Securities Act of 1933, the Securities Exchange Act of 1934, the Trust Indenture Act of 1939, the Investment Company Act of 1940, or the Investment Advisers Act of 1940, or any rule or regulation under any of these statutes; or (ii) the laws of the State in which the issuer maintains its principal place of business or any State in which this notice is filed.

Certifying that, if the issuer is claiming a Regulation D exemption for the offering, the issuer is not disqualified from relying on Regulation D for one of the reasons stated in Rule 505(b)(2)(iii) or Rule 506(d).

* This undertaking does not affect any limits Section 102(a) of the National Securities Markets Improvement Act of 1996 ("NSMIA") [Pub. L. No. 104-290, 110 Stat. 3416 (Oct. 11, 1996)] imposes on the ability of States to require information. As a result, if the securities that are the subject of this Form D are "covered securities" for purposes of NSMIA, whether in all instances or due to the nature of the offering that is the subject of this Form D, States cannot routinely require offering materials under this undertaking or otherwise and can require offering materials only to the extent NSMIA permits them to do so under NSMIA's preservation of their anti-fraud authority.

Each identified issuer has read this notice, knows the contents to be true, and has duly caused this notice to be signed on its behalf by the undersigned duly authorized person. (Check this box ☐ and attach Signature Continuation Pages for signatures of issuers identified in Item 1 above but not represented by signer below.)

Issuer(s)

Name of Signer

Signature

Title

Date

Number of continuation pages attached:

Persons who respond to the collection of information contained in this form are not required to respond unless the form displays a currently valid OMB number.

FORM D

U.S. Securities and Exchange Commission
Washington, DC 20549

Instructions for Submitting a Form D Notice

General Instructions

Who must file: Each issuer of securities that sells its securities in reliance on an exemption provided in Regulation D or Section 4(a)(5) of the Securities Act of 1933 must file this notice containing the information requested with the U.S. Securities and Exchange Commission (SEC) and with the state(s) requiring it. If more than one issuer has sold its securitie in the same transaction, all issuers should be identified in one filing with the SEC, but some states may require a separate filing for each issuer or security sold.

When to file:

o An issuer must file a new notice with the SEC for each new offering of securities no later than 15 calendar days after the "date of first sale" of securities in the offering as explained in the Instruction to Item 7. For this purpose, the date of first sale is the date on which the first investor is irrevocably contractually committed to invest, which, depending on the terms and conditions of the contract, could be the date on which the issuer receives the investor's subscription agreement or check. An issuer may file the notice at any time before that if it has determined to make the offering. An issuer must file a new notice with each state that requires it at the time set by the state. For state filing information, go to www.NASAA.org. A mandatory capital commitment call does not constitute a new offering, but is made under the original offering, so no new Form D filing is required.

o An issuer may file an amendment to a previously filed notice at any time.

o An issuer must file an amendment to a previously filed notice for an offering:

- to correct a material mistake of fact or error in the previously filed notice, as soon as practicable after discovery of the mistake or error;

- to reflect a change in the information provided in the previously filed notice, except as provided below, as soon as practicable after the change; and

- annually, on or before the first anniversary of the most recent previously filed notice, if the offering is continuing at that time.

When amendment is not required: An issuer is not required to file an amendment to a previously filed notice to reflect a change that occurs after the offering terminates or a change that occurs solely in the following information:

- the address or relationship to the issuer of a related person identified in response to Item 3;

- an issuer's revenues or aggregate net asset value;

- the minimum investment amount, if the change is an increase, or if the change, together with all other changes in that amount since the previously filed notice, does not result in a decrease of more than 10%;

- any address or state(s) of solicitation shown in response to Item 12;

- the total offering amount, if the change is a decrease, or if the change, together with all other changes in that amount since the previously filed notice, does not result in an increase of more than 10%;

- the amount of securities sold in the offering or the amount remaining to be sold;

- the number of non-accredited investors who have invested in the offering, as long as the change does not increase the number to more than 35;

- the total number of investors who have invested in the offering; and

- the amount of sales commissions, finders' fees or use of proceeds for payments to executive officers, directors or promoters, if the change is a decrease, or if the change, together with all other changes in that amount since the previously filed notice, does not result in an increase of more than 10%.

Saturdays, Sundays and holidays: If the date on which a notice or an amendment to a previously filed notice is required to be filed falls on a Saturday, Sunday or holiday, the due date is the first business day following.

Amendment content: An issuer that files an amendment to a previously filed notice must provide current information in response to all items of this Form D, regardless of why the amendment is filed.

How to file: Issuers must file this notice with the SEC in electronic format. For state filing information, go to www.NASAA.org.

Filing fee: There is no federal fiing fee. For information on state filing fees, go to www.NASAA.org.

Definitions of terms: Terms used but not defined in this form that are defined in Rule 405 and Rule 501 under the Securities Act of 1933, 17 CFR 230.405 and 230.501, have the meanings given to them in those rules.

FORM D

Item-by-Item Instructions

Item 1. Issuer's Identity. Identify each legal entity issuing any securities being reported as being offered by entering its full name; any previous name used within the past five years; and its jurisdiction of incorporation or organization, type of legal entity, and year of incorporation or organization within the past five years or status as formed over five years ago or not yet formed. If more than one entity is issuing the securities, identify a primary issuer in the first fields shown on the first page of the form, checking the box provided, and identify additional issuers by attaching Items 1 and 2 continuation page(s).

Item 2. Principal Place of Business and Contact Information. Enter a full street address of the issuer's principal place of business. Post office box numbers and "In care of" addresses are not acceptable. Enter a contact telephone number for the issuer. If you identified more than one issuer in response to Item 1, enter the requested information for the primary issuer you identified in response to that item and, at your option, for any or all of the other issuers you identified on your Item 1 and 2 continuation page(s).

Item 3. Related Persons. Enter the full name and address of each person having the specified relationships with any issuer and identify each relationship:

- Each executive officer and director of the issuer and person performing similar functions (title alone is not determinative) for the issuer, such as the general and managing partners of partnerships and managing members of limited liability companies; and

- Each person who has functioned directly or indirectly as a promoter of the issuer within the past five years of the later of the first sale of securities or the date upon which the Form D filing was required to be made.

If necessary to prevent the information supplied from being misleading, also provide a clarification in the space provided.

Identify additional persons having the specified relationships by checking the box provided and attaching Item 3 continuation page(s).

Item 4. Industry Group. Select the issuer's industry group. If the issuer or issuers can be categorized in more than one industry group, select the industry group that most accurately reflects the use of the bulk of the proceeds of the offering. For purposes of this filing, use the ordinary dictionary and commonly understood meanings of the terms identifying the industry group.

Item 5. Issuer Size.

- **Revenue Range** (for issuers that do not specify "Hedge Fund" or "Other Investment Fund" in response to Item 4): Enter the revenue range of the issuer or of all the issuers together for the most recently completed fiscal year available, or, if not in existence for a fiscal year, revenue range to date. Domestic SEC reporting companies should state revenues in accordance with Regulation S-X under the Securities Exchange Act of 1934. Domestic non-reporting companies should state revenues in accordance with U.S. Generally Accepted Accounting Principles (GAAP). Foreign issuers should calculate revenues in U.S. dollars and state them in accordance with U.S. GAAP, home country GAAP or International Financial Reporting Standards. If the issuer(s) declines to disclose its revenue range, enter "Decline to Disclose." If the issuer's(s') business is intended to produce revenue but did not, enter "No Revenues." If the business is not intended to produce revenue (for example, the business seeks asset appreciation only), enter "Not Applicable."

- **Aggregate Net Asset Value** (for issuers that specify "Hedge Fund" or "Other Investment Fund" in response to Item 4): Enter the aggregate net asset value range of the issuer or of all the issuers together as of the most recent practicable date. If the issuer(s) declines to disclose its aggregate net asset value range, enter "Decline to Disclose."

Item 6. Federal Exemption(s) and Exclusion(s) Claimed. Select the provision(s) being claimed to exempt the offering and resulting sales from the federal registration requirements under the Securities Act of 1933 and, if applicable, to exclude the issuer from the definition of "investment company" under the Investment Company Act of 1940. Select "Rule 504(b)(1) (not (i), (ii) or (iii))" only if the issuer is relying on the exemption in the introductory sentence of Rule 504 for offers and sales that satisfy all the terms and conditions of Rules 501 and 502(a), (c) and (d).

Item 7. Type of Filing. Indicate whether the issuer is filing a new notice or an amendment to a notice that was filed previously. If this is a new notice, enter the date of the first sale of securities in the offering or indicate that the first sale has "Yet to Occur." For this purpose, the date of first sale is the date on which the first investor is irrevocably contractually committed to invest, which, depending on the terms and conditions of the contract, could be the date on which the issuer receives the investor's subscription agreement or check.

Item 8. Duration of Offering. Indicate whether the issuer intends the offering to last for more than one year.

FORM D

Item-by-Item Instructions (Continued)

Item 9. Type(s) of Securities Offered. Select the appropriate type or types of securities offered as to which this notice is filed. If the securities are debt convertible into other securities, however, select "Debt" and any other appropriate types of securities except for "Equity." For purposes of this filing, use the ordinary dictionary and commonly understood meanings of these categories. For instance, equity securities would be securities that represent proportional ownership in an issuer, such as ordinary common and preferred stock of corporations and partnership and limited liability company interests; debt securities would be securities representing money loaned to an issuer that must be repaid to the investor at a later date; pooled investment fund interests would be securities that represent ownership interests in a pooled or collective investment vehicle; tenant-in-common securities would be securities that include an undivided fractional interest in real property other than a mineral property; and mineral property securities would be securities that include an undivided interest in an oil, gas or other mineral property.

Item 10. Business Combination Transaction. Indicate whether or not the offering is being made in connection with a business combination, such as an exchange (tender) offer or a merger, acquisition, or other transaction of the type described in paragraph (a)(1), (2) or (3) of Rule 145 under the Securities Act of 1933. Do not include an exchange (tender) offer for a class of the issuer's own securities. If necessary to prevent the information supplied from being misleading, also provide a clarification in the space provided.

Item 11. Minimum Investment. Enter the minimum dollar amount of investment that will be accepted from any outside investor. If the offering provides a minimum investment amount for outside investors that can be waived, provide the lowest amount below which a waiver will not be granted. If there is no minimum investment amount, enter "0." Investors will be considered outside investors if they are not employees, officers, directors, general partners, trustees (where the issuer is a business trust), consultants, advisors or vendors of the issuer, its parents, its majority owned subsidiaries, or majority owned subsidiaries of the issuer's parent.

Item 12. Sales Compensation. Enter the requested information for each person that has been or will be paid directly or indirectly any commission or other similar compensation in cash or other consideration in connection with sales of securities in the offering, including finders. Enter the CRD number for every person identified and any broker and dealer listed that has a CRD number. CRD numbers can be found at http://brokercheck.finra.org. A person that does not have a CRD number need not obtain one in order to be listed, and must be listed when required regardless of whether the person has a CRD number. In addition, check the State(s) in which the named person has solicited or intends to solicit investors. If more than five persons to be listed are associated persons of the same broker or dealer, enter only the name of the broker or dealer, its CRD number and street address, and the State(s) in which the named person has solicited or intends to solicit investors.

Item 13. Offering and Sales Amounts. Enter the dollar amount of securities being offered under a claim of federal exemption identified in Item 6 above. Also enter the dollar amount of securities sold in the offering as of the filing date. Select the "Indefinite" box if the amount being offered is undetermined or cannot be calculated at the present time, such as if the offering includes securities to be acquired upon the exercise or exchange of other securities or property and the exercise price or exchange value is not currently known or knowable. If an amount is definite but difficult to calculate without unreasonable effort or expense, provide a good faith estimate. The total offering and sold amounts should include all cash and other consideration to be received for the securities, including cash to be paid in the future under mandatory capital commitments. In offerings for consideration other than cash, the amounts entered should be based on the issuer's good faith valuation of the consideration. If necessary to prevent the information supplied from being misleading, also provide a clarification in the space provided.

Item 14. Investors. Indicate whether securities in the offering have been or may be sold to persons who do not qualify as accredited investors as defined in Rule 501(a), 17 CFR 230.501(a), and provide the number of such investors who have already invested in the offering. In addition, regardless of whether securities in the offering have been or may be sold to persons who do not qualify as accredited investors, specify the total number of investors who already have invested.

Item 15. Sales Commission and Finders' Fees Expenses. The information on sales commissions and finders' fees expenses may be given as subject to future contingencies.

Item 16. Use of Proceeds. No additional instructions.

Signature and Submission. An individual who is a duly authorized representative of each issuer identified must sign, date and submit this notice for the issuer. The capacity in which the individual is signing should be set forth in the "Title" field underneath the individual's name.

The name of the issuer(s) on whose behalf the notice is being submitted should be set forth in the "Issuer" field beside the individual's name; if the individual is signing on behalf of all issuers submitting the notice, the word "All" may be set forth in the "Issuer" field. Attach signature continuation page(s) to have different individuals sign on behalf of different issuer(s). Enter the number of continuation pages attached and included in the filing. If no continuation pages are attached, enter "0".

FORM D

U.S. Securities and Exchange Commission
Washington, DC 20549
Items 1 and 2 Continuation Page

Item 1 and 2. Issuer's Identity and Contact Information (Continued)

Name of Issuer

Jurisdiction of Incorporation/Organization

Previous Name(s) ☐ None

Entity Type (Select one)
- ○ Corporation
- ○ Limited Partnership
- ○ Limited Liability Company
- ○ General Partnership
- ○ Business Trust
- ○ Other (Specify)

Year of Incorporation/Organization
(Select one)
○ Over Five Years Ago ○ Within Last Five Years (specify year) ○ Yet to Be Formed

At your option, supply separate contact information for this issuer:

Street Address 1 | Street Address 2

City | State/Province/Country | ZIP/Postal Code | Phone No.

Name of Issuer

Jurisdiction of Incorporation/Organization

Previous Name(s) ☐ None

Entity Type (Select one)
- ○ Corporation
- ○ Limited Partnership
- ○ Limited Liability Company
- ○ General Partnership
- ○ Business Trust
- ○ Other (Specify)

Year of Incorporation/Organization
(Select one)
○ Over Five Years Ago ○ Within Last Five Years (specify year) ○ Yet to Be Formed

At your option, supply separate contact information for this issuer:

Street Address 1 | Street Address 2

City | State/Province/Country | ZIP/Postal Code | Phone No.

Name of Issuer

Jurisdiction of Incorporation/Organization

Previous Name(s) ☐ None

Entity Type (Select one)
- ○ Corporation
- ○ Limited Partnership
- ○ Limited Liability Company
- ○ General Partnership
- ○ Business Trust
- ○ Other (Specify)

Year of Incorporation/Organization
(Select one)
○ Over Five Years Ago ○ Within Last Five Years (specify year) ○ Yet to Be Formed

At your option, supply separate contact information for this issuer:

Street Address 1 | Street Address 2

City | State/Province/Country | ZIP/Postal Code | Phone No.

(Copy and use additional copies of this page as necessary.)

FORM D

U.S. Securities and Exchange Commission

Washington, DC 20549

Item 3 Continuation Page

Item 3. Related Persons (Continued)

Last Name　First Name　Middle Name

Street Address 1　Street Address 2

City　State/Province/Country　ZIP/Postal Code

Relationship(s): ☐ Executive Officer ☐ Director ☐ Promoter

Clarification of Response (if necessary)

Last Name　First Name　Middle Name

Street Address 1　Street Address 2

City　State/Province/Country　ZIP/Postal Code

Relationship(s): ☐ Executive Officer ☐ Director ☐ Promoter

Clarification of Response (if necessary)

Last Name　First Name　Middle Name

Street Address 1　Street Address 2

City　State/Province/Country　ZIP/Postal Code

Relationship(s): ☐ Executive Officer ☐ Director ☐ Promoter

Clarification of Response (if necessary)

Last Name　First Name　Middle Name

Street Address 1　Street Address 2

City　State/Province/Country　ZIP/Postal Code

Relationship(s): ☐ Executive Officer ☐ Director ☐ Promoter

Clarification of Response (if necessary)

(Copy and use additional copies of this page as necessary.)

FORM D

U.S. Securities and Exchange Commission
Washington, DC 20549

Item 12 Continuation Page

Item 12. Sales Compensation (Continued)

Recipient

Recipient CRD Number

☐ No CRD Number

(Associated) Broker or Dealer ☐ None

(Associated) Broker or Dealer CRD Number

☐ No CRD Number

Street Address 1

Street Address 2

City

State/Province/Country

ZIP/Postal Code

States of Solicitation ☐ All States

☐ AL ☐ AK ☐ AZ ☐ AR ☐ CA ☐ CO ☐ CT ☐ DE ☐ DC ☐ FL ☐ GA ☐ HI ☐ ID
☐ IL ☐ IN ☐ IA ☐ KS ☐ KY ☐ LA ☐ ME ☐ MD ☐ MA ☐ MI ☐ MN ☐ MS ☐ MO
☐ MT ☐ NE ☐ NV ☐ NH ☐ NJ ☐ NM ☐ NY ☐ NC ☐ ND ☐ OH ☐ OK ☐ OR ☐ PA
☐ RI ☐ SC ☐ SD ☐ TN ☐ TX ☐ UT ☐ VT ☐ VA ☐ WA ☐ WV ☐ WI ☐ WY ☐ PR

Recipient

Recipient CRD Number

☐ No CRD Number

(Associated) Broker or Dealer ☐ None

(Associated) Broker or Dealer CRD Number

☐ No CRD Number

Street Address 1

Street Address 2

City

State/Province/Country

ZIP/Postal Code

States of Solicitation ☐ All States

☐ AL ☐ AK ☐ AZ ☐ AR ☐ CA ☐ CO ☐ CT ☐ DE ☐ DC ☐ FL ☐ GA ☐ HI ☐ ID
☐ IL ☐ IN ☐ IA ☐ KS ☐ KY ☐ LA ☐ ME ☐ MD ☐ MA ☐ MI ☐ MN ☐ MS ☐ MO
☐ MT ☐ NE ☐ NV ☐ NH ☐ NJ ☐ NM ☐ NY ☐ NC ☐ ND ☐ OH ☐ OK ☐ OR ☐ PA
☐ RI ☐ SC ☐ SD ☐ TN ☐ TX ☐ UT ☐ VT ☐ VA ☐ WA ☐ WV ☐ WI ☐ WY ☐ PR

(Copy and use additional copies of this page as necessary.)

FORM D

U.S. Securities and Exchange Commission
Washington, DC 20549

Signature Continuation Page

Signature and Submission

The undersigned is the duly authorized representative of the issuer(s), identied in the field beside the individual's name below.

Issuer

Name of Signer

Signature

Title

Date

Issuer

Name of Signer

Signature

Title

Date

Issuer

Name of Signer

Signature

Title

Date

Issuer

Name of Signer

Signature

Title

Date

(Copy and use additional copies of this page as necessary.)

Sample New York Regulation D Rule 506 Notice of Exemption

OFFICE OF ATTORNEY GENERAL ERIC T. SCHNEIDERMAN File # _____

STATE OF NEW YORK DEPARTMENT OF LAW

NY FORM 99

INVESTOR PROTECTION BUREAU / REAL ESTATE FINANCE BUREAU

NOTIFICATION FILING

Pursuant to National Securities Markets Improvement Act of 1996 ("NSMIA")

Submission to: INVESTOR PROTECTION BUREAU ("IPB") Securities Theatrical Syndications

REAL ESTATE FINANCE BUREAU ("REF")

Type of Filing: New Filing

Amendment or Renewal (If name, address or offering has changed, indicate change):

A. BASIC IDENTIFICATION DATA

Full Name of Issuer (and Theatrical Production Company, if applicable):

Address of Executive Offices: Telephone Number ( ) _____ - _________

(Number and Street) (City or Town) (State & ZIP)

Type of Organization: business corporation limited liability company limited partnership not-for-profit corporation business trust political subdivision of state common fund state agency or authority county, city, town or village (agency, authority or instrumentality corporation) other (specify):

Category of "Covered Security" (NSMIA):

Offering to "Qualified Purchasers" [1933 Act* §18(b)(3)]

Rule 506 Offering [1933 Act* § 4(2) - per §18(b)(4)(D)]

Other qualifying offering (specify):

* Securities Act of 1933, as amended

The Securities Will Be Sold By: officers or directors of issuer salespersons employed by issuer officers or directors of an affiliated person underwriter, dealer or broker registered in New York

For Theatrical Syndication Offerings, add the following information:

Name of proposed production:

Location of production:

Proposed opening date:

IPB099 - (rev. 5/12)

B. INFORMATION ABOUT OFFERING

Total Offering Amount (maximum) $___________ Minimum Offering Amount $_____________

Type of Security Offered (brief description):

Enclosures (add additional sheets if necessary):

☐ Copy of Consent to Service of Process (U-2) (original to New York State Department of State, Albany NY)
☐ Offering Documents
☐ Confidential Attachment to Form 99
☐ Further information as to ☐ issuer ☐ affiliated persons
☐ Form D: ☐ copy "as filed" with the S.E.C ☐ "as filed" copy will follow
☐ Theatrical Venture Amendment - Required Supplemental Information

C. INFORMATION ABOUT ISSUER, PRINCIPALS AND CONTROLLING PERSONS

• **As to issuer:**

1. Is issuer subject to or a respondent in any legal action for, any injunction, cease-and-desist order or order or stipulation to desist or refrain from any act or practice relating to the offering of securities in New York or any other jurisdiction? . . . . ☐ Yes ☐ No
2. (a) Has issuer ever been convicted of or pleaded guilty to any crime (i) involving any fraud, or (ii) relating to any financial transaction or handling of funds of another person, or (iii) pertaining to any dealings in any securities? . . . . ☐ Yes ☐ No

   (b) Is issuer now a defendant in any such criminal proceeding? . . . . ☐ Yes ☐ No

• **As to each Principal*, each Controlling Person, and any Sponsoring Entity of issuer:**

3. Is any one of the above subject to or a respondent in any legal action for, any injunction, cease-and-desist order or order or stipulation to desist or refrain from any act or practice relating to the offering of securities in New York or any other jurisdiction? . . . . ☐ Yes ☐ No

4. (a) Has any one of the above ever been convicted of or pleaded guilty to any crime (i) involving any fraud, or (ii) relating to any financial transaction or handling of funds of another person, or (iii) pertaining to any dealings in any securities? . . . . ☐ Yes ☐ No

   (b) Is any one of the above now a defendant in any such criminal proceeding ? . . . . ☐ Yes ☐ No

5. Has any of the above ever been suspended or expelled from membership in any securities or commodities exchange or association or had a securities or commodities license or registration denied, suspended or revoked? . . . . ☐ Yes ☐ No

6. Has any of the above been a controlling person or sponsor with respect to any issuer which engaged in a distribution of securities or any public offering within the past three (3) years? . . . . ☐ Yes ☐ No

If the answer to any of the above is "yes", give material facts on an attached sheet.

* Capitalized terms are defined in Section E of Form 99.

D. CERTIFICATION

The undersigned affirms and certifies, to his or her knowledge and belief after due investigation and inquiry, and under penalty of perjury, that any and all information provided in this Form 99 is true and complete, and that there are no misrepresentations, omissions or untruths contained herein. The undersigned further understands and intends that the information supplied in this Form will be relied upon by the New York State Department of Law and that any false statement made herein is punishable as a Class A misdemeanor under New York Penal Law §175.30, §210.45, or both.

Dated: ______________________, 20 ____

Issuer (name of entity): ______________________

By: ______________________
Authorized Principal or Controlling Person

Print Name: ______________________

Title or Affiliation: ______________________

CONFIDENTIAL ATTACHMENT TO FORM 99
(Social Security numbers and residential information will be held strictly confidential)

Issuer Name: ____

Form 99 dated: ____________________, 20 ___

ACCESS TO THE FOLLOWING INFORMATION WILL BE
WITHHELD PURSUANT TO NEW YORK PUBLIC OFFICERS LAW ("FOIL") §89(2)(b):

Identity of Principals (i) of issuer, (ii) of Controlling Person(s)* and (iii) of Sponsoring Entity:

Name	**Date of Birth**	**Social Security Number**
____________________	____________________	____________________
____________________	____________________	____________________
____________________	____________________	____________________
____________________	____________________	____________________
____________________	____________________	____________________
____________________	____________________	____________________
____________________	____________________	____________________
____________________	____________________	____________________
____________________	____________________	____________________
____________________	____________________	____________________

*Capitalized terms are defined in Section E of Form 99.

E. INSTRUCTIONS

1. General Instructions.

Who May File: All persons engaging in an offering of or transaction in securities within or from New York which are defined as "covered securities" (other than "listed securities" or open-end management type companies registered with the S.E.C. under the Investment Company Act of 1940 (the "1940 Act") under §18 of the 1933 Act as amended by NSMIA. No filing is required for listed securities. Open-end management type companies registered within the S.E.C. under the 1940 Act must file Form NF; other registered investment companies may file Form NF instead of Form 99. An issuer entitled to submit a Notification Filing for transactions, not involving real estate securities, may elect to file instead with IP an M-11 Issuer Statement under GBL §359-e or an application for exemption under §359-f(2).

Where To File: Address for both Bureaus - 120 Broadway, 23rd Floor, New York, NY 10271

(a) **IP if:**

(i) within New York General Business Law ("GBL") §359-e
(ii) within ACAL §23.03 et seq.

(b) **REF if:**

(iii) real estate securities or other securities deemed within purview of GBL §352-e or §352-g

When To File: Prior to any sale or offer for sale of securities in or from New York. For theatrical ventures, supplemental statements (in the form of Amendment to Form 99) must be filed advising the Department of Law of (i) date of the first expenditure of investors' funds, and (ii) date of the last public performance, if any, of the original production in New York State. Such Amendment must be submitted within ten (10) business days of the occurrence.

Copies Required: Two (2) copies of Form 99 must be filed, one of which must be manually signed, along with a photocopy of the manually signed copy. One (1) copy of the Offering Documents must also be filed.

Information Required: A new filing must contain all information requested. Amendments require only notification of changes with respect to information given in Form 99.

Form D: In addition to Form 99, submit a copy of Form D as filed. In the event that Form D has not yet been filed with the S.E.C., submit a copy of the unfiled Form D and provide information as to when such filing will be effected ("as filed" copy must be submitted when so filed).

Non-Resident Issuers: Consent to Service of Process must be filed with the Department of State, 99 Washington Avenue, Albany, NY 12231; a copy must be filed with Form 99.

Effect of Filing: A Notification Filing is deemed made when received at the address given on Form 99. In the event that the information given in the Notification Filing is incomplete, or conflicts with or is otherwise inconsistent with other information in the possession of Department of Law, the issuer will be notified. Notification Filings shall not be effective for the following offerings or transactions:

(a) Any offering wherein the issuer, or its Controlling Person(s) or its Sponsor(s), or one or more of its Principals, or one or more principals of a Controlling Person or a Sponsor (i) are, or during the past six years have been, enjoined from the offer or sale of securities within or from the State of New York, or (ii) have entered into a stipulation or consent, which remains currently in effect, to desist or refrain from making offers of sales of securities within or from the State of New York unless and until the Attorney General makes a determination that these facts or circumstances do not appear to amount to a violation of such prior judgment, order or stipulation, or do not themselves constitute a violation of GBL Article 23-A, or that such action as to the Form 99 filing is not necessary to protect the public interest; and

(b) Offerings of securities which constitute cooperative interests in realty requiring a full filing under GBL §352-e.

2. Definitions.

The terms set forth below shall be defined as follows for purposes of completing this Form 99:

(a) **Controlling Person** shall mean: Every person who, by or through stock ownership, agency, or otherwise, or who, pursuant to or in connection with an agreement or understanding with one or more other persons by or through stock ownership, agency, or otherwise, controls any person liable under §11 or §12 of the 1933 Act, as amended.

(b) **Offering Documents** shall mean: Any printed materials in which is presented, without limitation, the terms of the transaction, a description of the securities offered, the operative documents for the entity which may be formed, any supporting documents and/or the subscription instruments for the investor.

(c) **Principal** or **principals** shall mean: One or more (i) general partners of a partnership, (ii) managing members of a limited liability company, (iii) trustees of a trust, (iv) managing directors of an association or other organization, (v) directors of a corporation who hold or control 10% or more of its voting shares or who are also officers, (vi) the six highest-ranking officers of a corporation, association or similar entity, including the chief executive officer, the chief operating officer, the chief financial officer, the chief legal officer, and the three highest-ranking vice-presidents (including any previously referred to), (vii) individuals or entities holding 33% or more of the voting equity interest in an entity, **and/or** (viii) individuals who have the status of a person in one or more of the previous clauses with respect to any entity that itself is a principal of the issuer.

(d) **Sponsor** or **Sponsoring Entity** shall mean: One or more individuals or entities (i) for whose account or benefit, indirect or otherwise, an issue of securities or an issuer has been created or originated, or (ii) who or which has a proprietary interest in and who directs or takes an active role in the creation, origination or promotion of the issuer or in the acquisition of business activities, business property or investment portfolio items thereof, but excluding attorneys, accountants, engineers, architects, appraisers, real estate brokers, property managers or other contractors or professionals performing services for contractual compensation.

3. Filing Fees: Payment should be made by check or money order to "New York State Department of Law" in accordance with GBL §352-e(7)(a) and §359-e(5), or the following schedule may be used:

Real Estate Syndications	
Fee Amount	Offering or Transaction
$1,050	under GBL §352-e and §359-e $500,000 or less offering amount
$1,950	under GBL §352-e and §359-e more than $500,000 offering amount
$750	under GBL §352-e no GBL §359-e registration
$300	under GBL §359-f(2) per GBL §352-e
Securities Transactions	
$1,200	under GBL §359-e more than $500,000 offering amount effective for four (4) years
$300	under GBL §359-e $500,000 or less offering amount effective for four (4) years
$30	for an amendment
Theatrical Syndications	
$0	under ACAL §23.03 et seq.

Sample New York Selling Agent Registration

NYS DEPARTMENT OF STATE
MISCELLANEOUS RECORDS BUREAU

ONE COMMERCE PLAZA, 99 WASHINGTON AVENUE
ALBANY, NY 12231-0001

This form constitutes TWO DISTINCT NOTICES, each of which must be filed in DUPLICATE. A fee of $75 must accompany **each** State Notice and **each** Further State Notice. Checks, money orders and bank drafts should be made payable to **Department of State**; amounts over $500 must be paid by money order, bank draft or certified check. Mail completed form and fee to the Miscellaneous Records Bureau at the above address. Please do not send cash through the mail.

DO NOT send offering literature to the Secretary of State.

State Notice *Under §359-e, subd. 2 of the General Business Law of the State of New York*

(FEE: $75 / State Notice. This notice must be filed by every security broker or dealer prior to engaging in the business of selling or offering for sale securities to the public in the State of New York.)

NAME OF DEALER OR BROKER

LIST BUSINESS OR POST OFFICE ADDRESS and "X" TYPE BELOW

"X" ONE
- ☐ BUSINESS ADDRESS
- ☐ POST OFFICE/MAILING ADDRESS

IF A CORPORATION, STATE OR COUNTRY IN WHICH INCORPORATED

IF A PARTNERSHIP, THE NAMES OF THE GENERAL PARTNERS

Further State Notice *Under §359-e, subd. 8 of the General Business Law of the State of New York*

(FEE: $75/Further State Notice. This notice to be filed for each issue to be offered, except those specifically exempted by §359-f.)

NAME OF DEALER, BROKER OR SYNDICATE MANAGER

LIST BUSINESS OR POST OFFICE ADDRESS and "X" TYPE BELOW

"X" ONE
- ☐ BUSINESS ADDRESS
- ☐ POST OFFICE/MAILING ADDRESS

IF A CORPORATION, STATE OR COUNTRY IN WHICH INCORPORATED

NAME OF SECURITY OR SECURITIES (CLASS)

NAME OF ISSUER OF SECURITIES

MAIL ADDRESS FOR ISSUER OF SECURITIES (i.e., POSTAL ADDRESS)

STATE OR COUNTRY IN WHICH ORGANIZED

DOS-125 (Rev. 5/98)

NEW YORK STATE DEPARTMENT OF STATE

Instructions for Filing State and Further State Notices

Please be sure to check these areas before submitting State Notice and Further State Notices.

Fees

- The filing fee for a State Notice (top portion of the form) is $75.00.
- The filing fee for a Further State Notice (bottom portion of the form) is $75.00.
- If submitting both a State Notice and a Further State Notice (top and bottom portion of the form) the filing fee is $150.00.

  There is no additional fee for the duplicate copy(ies).

State Notice

(Top portion of form; must be filed in duplicate)

- Provide the name and address of the Dealer **OR** Broker. We cannot accept N/A in EITHER area. After registering as a Dealer or a Broker, you may act as a Syndicate Manager and file a Further State Notice as such. However, for the purposes of the State Notice, you act as either a Dealer or a Broker.
- If a corporation, indicate the state or country in which incorporated. If a partnership, leave the incorporation line blank and enter the names of the General Partners in the (next) section provided.
- **ONLY ONE NAME** is permitted per State Notice; e.g., if a Dealer and Broker will both be involved, two separate State Notices are required. If an exemption has been granted, please state such in the State Notice portion of the form.
- A State Notice is a one-time filing unless there has been a name or address change.

Further State Notice

(Bottom portion of form; must be filed in duplicate)

- Be sure that whomever you list as the Dealer, Broker **AND/OR** Syndicate Manager has a prior State Notice on file with the New York State Department of State as a Dealer or Broker.
- Provide the name and address for each Dealer, Broker and/or Syndicate Manager. We cannot accept N/A in EITHER area.
- If a corporation, indicate the state or country in which incorporated. If a partnership, leave the incorporation line blank and enter the names of the General Partners in the (next) section provided.
- If more than one Dealer, Broker or Syndicate Manager is involved, list the names, addresses and where incorporated for each. Preferably, place a (corresponding) number in parentheses next to each name, address and incorporation.
- List the class of security to be offered. We cannot accept multiple classes on one Further State Notice form, *unless* they are preceded by "Units consisting of ..." or "Common stock **with** warrants," etc. Please be advised that the word **"and"** denotes multiple filings. Also, do *not* list Fund names as classes of securities; we need to know what (in the fund) is being offered; i.e., "Shares of Beneficial Interest," etc.
- Provide the Issuer's name and address as well as where organized. **Only ONE Issuer name** is permitted per Further State Notice.

Combination State and Further State Notice

- If submitting a State Notice for a Dealer or Broker who will be offering the securities for the Issuer named on the Further State Notice (below), the names must match exactly on both forms; e.g., do not list the Broker as "ABC Fund" on the State Notice and "ABC Fund/ABC Senior Managed Portfolio" on the Further State Notice.

NOTICE: We cannot alter forms or filings received by this office. If an error is made that requires a revision to the form or filing, it will have to be resubmitted with the appropriate filing fee.

(REV 5/98)

Sample Uniform Consent to Service

Form U-2

Form U-2 Uniform Consent to Service of Process

KNOW ALL MEN BY THESE PRESENTS:

That the undersigned ______________________________ (a corporation), (a partnership), a () organized under the laws of ________________________ or (an individual), [strike out inapplicable nomenclature] for purposes of complying with the laws of the States indicated hereunder relating to either the registration or sale of securities, hereby irrevocably appoints the officers of the States so designated hereunder and their successors in such offices, its attorney in those States so designated upon whom may be served any notice, process or pleading in any action or proceeding against it arising out of, or in connection with, the sale of securities or out of violation of the aforesaid laws of the States so designated; and the undersigned does hereby consent that any such action or proceeding against it may be commenced in any court of competent jurisdiction and proper venue within the States so designated hereunder by service of process upon the officers so designated with the same effect as if the undersigned was organized or created under the laws of that State and have been served lawfully with process in that State.

It is requested that a copy of any notice, process or pleading served hereunder be mailed to:

____

(Name)

____

(Address)

Place an "X" before the names of all the States for which the person executing this form is appointing the designated Officer of each State as its attorney in that State for receipt of service of process:

___AL	Secretary of State	__FL	Dept. of Banking and Finance
___AK	Administrator of the Division of Banking and Corporations, Department of Commerce and Economic Development	__GA	Commissioner of Securities
___AZ	The Corporation Commission	___GUAM	Administrator, Department of Finance
___AR	The Securities Commissioner	___HI	Commissioner of Securities
___CA	Commissioner of Corporations	___ID	Director, Department of Finance
___CO	Securities Commissioner	___IL	Secretary of State
___CT	Banking Commissioner	___IN	Secretary of State
___DE	Securities Commissioner	___IA	Commissioner of Insurance
___DC	Dept. of Insurance, Securities and Banking	___KS	Secretary of State
___KY	Director, Division of Securities	___OH	Secretary of State
___LA	Commissioner of Securities	___OR	Director, Department of

			Insurance and Finance
___ME	Administrator, Securities Division	___OK	Securities Administrator
___MD	Commissioner of the Division of Securities	___PA	Pennsylvania does not require filing of a Consent to Service of Process
___MA	Secretary of State	___PR	Commissioner of Financial Institutions
___MI	Commissioner, Office of Financial and Insurance Services	___RI	Director of Business Regulation
___MN	Commissioner of Commerce	___SC	Securities Commissioner
___MS	Secretary of State	___SD	Director of the Division of Securities
___MO	Securities Commissioner	___TN	Commissioner of Commerce and Insurance
___MT	State Auditor and Commissioner of Insurance	___TX	Securities Commissioner
___NE	Director of Banking and Finance	___UT	Director, Division of Securities
___NV	Secretary of State	___VT	Commissioner of Banking, Insurance, Securities & Health Administration
___NH	Secretary of State	___VA	Clerk, State Corporation Commission
___NJ	Chief, Securities Bureau	___WA	Director of the Department of Licensing
		___WV	Commissioner of Securities
___NM	Director, Securities Division		
___NY	Secretary of State	___WI	Department of Financial Institutions, Division of Securities
___NC	Secretary of State	___WY	Secretary of State
___ND	Securities Commissioner		

Dated this_________________________________ day of ________________________, 20___
(SEAL)

____

By __________________________________

____

Title

INSTRUCTIONS TO FORM U-2
UNIFORM CONSENT TO SERVICE OF PROCESS

1. The name of the issuer is to be inserted in the blank space on line 1 Uniform Form U-2 ("Form").

2. The type of person executing the Form is to be described by striking out the inapplicable nomenclature in lines 2-4 and, if appropriate, by inserting a description of the person in the blank space provided on line 2 of the Form.

3. The name of the jurisdiction under which the issuer was formed or is to be formed is to be inserted in the blank spaces on line 3 of the Form.

4. The person to whom a copy of any notice, process of pleading which is served pursuant to the Consent to Service of Process is to be inserted in the appropriate black spaces at the end of page 1 of the Form.

5. An "X" is to be placed in the space before the names of all States which the person executing this Form lawfully is appointing the officer of each State so designed on the Form as its attorney in that State for receipt of service of process.

6. A manually signed Form must be filed with each State requiring a Consent to Service of Process on Form U-2 at the office so designated by the laws or regulations of that State and must be accompanied by the exact filing fee, if any.

7. The Form must be signed by the issuer. If the issuer is a corporation, it should be signed in the name of the corporation by an executive officer duly authorized; if a partnership, it should be signed in the name of the partnership by a general partner; and if an unincorporated association or other organization which is not a partnership, the Form should be signed in the name of such organization by a person responsible for the direction of management of its affairs.

8. If the Form is mailed, it is advisable to send it by registered or certified mail, postage prepared, return receipt requested.

CORPORATE ACKNOWLEDGMENT

State or Province of_____________)
County of ________________________) ss.

On this ______ day of ____________, 20 _____ before me __________________ the undersigned officer, personally appeared ___________________________________ known personally to me to be the _________________ of the above named corporation and
(Title)
acknowledged that he, as an officer being authorized so to do, executed the foregoing instrument for the purposes therein contained, by signing the name of the corporation by himself as an officer.

IN WITNESS WHEREOF I have hereunto set my hand and official seal.

____
Notary Public/Commissioner of Oath
My Commission Expires________________

(SEAL)

INDIVIDUAL OR PARTNERSHIP ACKNOWLEDGMENT

State or Province of ___________)
County of _______________________) ss.

On this _______day of _____________, 20______, before me, ______________, the undersigned officer, personally appeared ____________________________ to me personally known and known to me to be the same person(s) whose name(s) is (are) signed to the foregoing instrument, and acknowledged the execution thereof for the uses and purposes therein set forth.

In WITNESS WHEREOF I have hereunto set my hand and official seal.

____
Notary Public/Commissioner of Oaths
My Commission Expires_____________

(SEAL)

INDEX